SMALL BUSINESS:
THEORY AND POLICY

Edited by Cyril Levicki

CROOM HELM

London & Sydney

© 1984 Acton Society Trust
Croom Helm Ltd, Provident House, Burrell Row,
Beckenham, Kent BR3 1AT
Croom Helm Australia Pty Ltd, GPO Box 5097,
Sydney, NSW 2001, Australia

British Library Cataloguing in Publication Data
Small business.
  1. Small business — Europe
  1. Levicki, Cyril II. Acton Society Trust
  338.6'094   HD2346.E9

Typeset by Photosetting & Secretarial Services Ltd.
Station Approach, Yeovil, Somerset. Tel: Yeovil 23684

Printed and bound in Great Britain by
Unwin Brothers Limited, The Gresham Press,
Old Woking, Surrey.

SMALL BUSINESS: THEORY AND POLICY

Contents

Acton Society

This book was sponsored by the Acton Society. The Acton Society Trust is an independent, non-profit making organisation, set up in 1948 as a recognised charitable trust. It takes its name from the nineteenth century historian, Lord Acton, who held that the justification of liberty lay in the realisation of human values. The Society has carried out or sponsored many research projects in economic and social fields.

A catalogue of the resulting publications is available from the **Acton Society, 9 Poland Street, London W1V 3DG (01 437 8954)**.

Notes on contributors

Julia Bamford is a lecturer in the Economics Department of Siena University, having previously taught at the University of Rome.

Pierre-Yves Barreyre is Professor of Management at Grenoble University. His book *Stratégie d'innovation dans les petites et moyennes industries* won the 'French Management Book of 1976' prize.

Michael Beesley is Professor of Economics at the London Business School. He is an authority on transport economics and has been a consultant to several governments. He is currently writing a textbook on managerial economics.

Dr. James Curran is Reader in Industrial Sociology at Kingston Polytechnic. Together with Professor John Stanworth, he is one of the pioneers of small business research in Britain.

Dr. Brian Hindley is senior lecturer at the London School of Economics. He has written publications on a wide range of economic themes.

Cyril Levicki has run his own small businesses and now teaches at the London Business School and at Queen Mary College.

Robin Marris is Professor and head of the Department of Economics at Birkbeck College, London University. His book *The economic theory of managerial capitalism* gave him an international reputation. He was formerly Professor of Economics, University of Maryland.

Ms. Pat Morrish is a lecturer at Birmingham and Aston Universities.

John M. Samuels is Professor of Business Finance at Birmingham University and currently also pro Vice-Chancellor. He has held a number of visiting appointments in the United States, and is author of several books on financial subjects, including *Mergers and takeovers* (1972) which he edited for the Acton Society.

Willibrord Sauer is head of the international relations division of the National Federation of German Skilled Crafts and Trades (ZDH) in Bonn and also Secretary-General of the European Association of Craft, Small and Medium-sized Enterprises in Brussels.

John Stanworth is Professor and Director of the Small Business Unit at the Polytechnic of Central London.

Dr. Michael Utton is Reader in Economics at Reading University, as well as consultant to the National Institute of Economic and Social Research. He has published several works on mergers, concentration and diversification, as well as *The Political Economy of Big Business*.

Peter Wilson is senior research officer at the London Business School, where he lectures on small business. He recently co-edited *New perspectives on small business*.

Introduction

Small business has become big news. In the somewhat frenetic turn and turnabout of fashion and trend in public policy-making, promotion of the merger mania of the 1960s has given way to an altogether different approach. The conventional wisdom no longer emphasises the need for ever bigger corporations in order to harness the economies of large-scale organisation, for now the stress is laid on the advantages of smaller units: divestment, management buy-outs, workers' co-ops, and encouragement for the individual entrepreneur are the current order of the day. This change of direction is welcomed by the Acton Society which, since its foundation in 1948, has endeavoured to examine the structures and organisation of work and government from the viewpoint of how they affect such human values as freedom and participation for the individual, both as a worker and as a citizen.

This book developed out of a series of seminars held in Siena in 1977 and 1979, which have continued on occasions since, both in Italy and in Britain. Among other themes, the seminars focused on an examination of the techniques needed to create successful small and skill-intensive units of organisation, and of identifying the problems standing in the way of developing these techniques. One such problem related to the economic and social consequences of the limited liability company, and this led to a book, *Limited Liability and the Corporation*, which appeared in 1982. It was followed by *The Nonconforming Radicals of Europe: the Future of Industrial Society*, published in 1983.

The present book concentrates exclusively on the issues affecting small business. It has three particular concerns: first to highlight the theoretical aspects of the subject; second to examine, in Britain and elsewhere, the economic conditions in which small firms exist; and third to trace the development of government policy towards small firms.

The book appears at a time of accelerating growth in the diverse provisions to support small enterprises. Mrs. Thatcher's government has pressing reasons for this policy: the Conservative party's commitment to encouraging individual initiative and enterprise, the need to move the country out of recession and the hope of reducing unemployment. According to the first issue (September, 1983) of the magazine *In Business Now*, sent free by the Department of Trade and

Industry to 'small and family businesses', there are 86 special schemes to help such firms. And the Small Firms Service of the Department listed more than a dozen measures in the 1983 Finance Act designed to encourage investment in small firms and reduce the burden of taxation on them. The Small Firm Service now has twelve regional information centres across the country and fifty area counselling offices.

And there are also the beginnings of a European dimension to small business support. The European Parliament having sponsored a series of conferences in each member country in 1983 ('the European Year of the Small and Medium Sized Enterprise') will in 1984 consider a report on the findings, and it is possible there will be new Community provisions to encourage small business. In October 1983 the Economic and Social Committee of the EEC, reporting on a proposal to empower the Commission to help finance innovation within the Community, concluded that more should be done to promote innovation among small and medium sized enterprises because 'existing measures are in general insufficient to provide conditions equivalent to those prevailing amongst the community's main competitors, Japan and the USA in particular'.

The UK organising committee of the European Year commissioned a 10-country comparative survey from the Economist Intelligence Unit. The preliminary results, heavily qualified by the lack of homogeneity in the collection of statistics in the different countries, suggest that the climate for small firms in Britain is in many respects less favourable than in most of the other EEC countries. In terms of tax incentives the UK scored more highly than any of the other countries, but British small and medium sized firms appear to be at a disadvantage in such matters as local taxation, capital availability, legislation to encourage competition, the costs of premises and the educational levels of the labour force. So the British government may come under pressure to review its policies and to find ways of removing more obstacles to the success of small business. The EEC committee noted that West Germany had the most comprehensive and effective measures. This book explains them in detail. It also raises the issue as to whether direct government intervention is the best way of meeting the real needs of the small businessman.

The final chapter of the book is a comprehensive survey of the research into small business and the authors make the point that the hopeful proposals and provisions that are now proliferating would be better directed if this research was more widely known and assimilated. A coherent and consistent public policy depends on well-founded research and this in turn depends on a purposeful direction of the research by the various academic and business institutions. The study of small business has yet to be established as a well-founded, legitimate field of academic concern *in its own right*. It is hoped that the publication of the present volume will help to enhance small business as a subject meriting systematic, long-term, scholarly investigation.

The editor would like to acknowledge the role of Edward Goodman, chairman of the Acton Society, who organised the original seminars and who over many years has sustained a deep interest in the study of scale and its consequences. He wishes to thank Peter Saynor, the director, for the final editing and shaping of the book and Gaenor Amory for her help in preparing it for publication.

Cyril Levicki

CHAPTER 1

Concentration, competition and the small firm[1]

M. A. Utton

I Introduction

One of the most dramatic changes in British industrial structure over the last 25 years or so has been the relative growth of the largest companies. According to the best estimates available, whereas the share of the 100 largest firms in manufacturing industry output increased only moderately in the first half of this century from 16% in 1909 to 22% in 1949, by 1976 it had practically doubled to 42.%[2] Although there are a number of indications that the upward trend may have slowed somewhat in the latter part of the 1970s it is still likely that in the near future half of manufacturing output in the UK will be produced by the 100 largest firms.

This sudden upsurge in the growth of the largest companies has meant that aggregate concentration in the manufacturing sector is now higher in the UK than in the US (where concentration was clearly higher until the mid-1950s and where it has remained relatively stable since about 1960) and probably higher than any other western industrialised economy. A particular characteristic of the growth of these companies has been in the number of separate plants they operate rather than in the expansion in the size of existing plants. Thus, whereas they operated an average of 27 plants each in 1958, this had grown more than $2\frac{1}{2}$ times to 72 each by 1972. This and the rising volume of merger activity in the late 1960s and early 1970s suggests that a considerable part of the increase in their share of the manufacturing sector output involved diversification of their activities across industries. One theme of this chapter is that the simultaneous occurrence of very high aggregate concentration with widespread diversification may have special implications for competition and the future of small (and even medium sized) firms. A further characteristic of these developments in the UK was, until comparatively recently, the endorsement by the government of the view that large size went hand in hand with efficiency and dynamism, so that for a period in the late 1960s a state body, the Industrial Reorganisation Corporation (IRC), was a leading agent in the creation of some of our most ponderous giants.

It is against this background that the main sections of this chapter are set. Section II examines in some detail the validity of the view that very large size has been the result mainly of a quest for efficiency. The recent evidence on this issue points rather in the opposite direction, in particular that efficiency in production in many industries probably requires nothing like the enormous size that the largest companies have now attained and further that beyond a certain size, other factors (like labour relations) may mean higher costs. On the other hand, factors which may have stimulated the growth of the largest firms, especially in marketing and finance, although producing private gains to the firms themselves, may be of dubious social value; ie they may either hinder moves to a more efficient allocation of resources or merely foster a permanent bias in favour of large firms. Not surprisingly while the largest firms were increasing their relative position so rapidly, firms at the other end of the distribution were losing out and one recent survey suggests that in the UK they now play a smaller part in the manufacturing sector than in any other Western economy.

Section III examines one result of the recent diversification by the largest firms: the extent of their penetration into industries remote from their previous experience. Of special concern is the spread of their activities into industries which have hitherto been considered largely the province of smaller firms and with the increasing encounters that the largest firms have with each other in these industries. Some writers have claimed that the competitive process may be irreparably damaged by the pricing strategies of large firms actively engaged across a wide spectrum of different industries. Although some of the more extravagant versions of this view may lack plausibility when set beside the available facts, there is very likely to be a long-run danger that the indirect effects of widespread diversification may lead to a deterioration in industrial performance.

The final section reviews the policy options that are available and makes some tentative suggestions for halting and perhaps reversing the trend towards massive size.

II Wisdom or delusion about efficiency and size?

When confronted by the enormous growth of the largest companies in the UK the most frequent response is likely to be that this is merely a reflection of the demands of modern technology. Technical economies of scale are so important, on this view, across a wide range of industries that to ignore them and insist on a fragmented industrial structure would be to condemn British industry to a much higher level of costs than is possible with present knowledge, and ensure a continued decline in our share of world exports. This view probably reached its apotheosis in the White Paper introducing the Industrial Reorganisation Corporation:

'The need for more concentration and rationalisation to promote the greater efficiency and international competitiveness of British industry ... is now widely recognised ... Many of the production units in this country are small by comparison with the most successful companies in international trade ... In some sectors the typical company in Britain is too small to achieve long production runs; to take advantage of economies of scale; undertake effective research and development; to support specialist departments for design and marketing; to install the most modern equipment or to attract the best qualified management'. *(1966, paras 2 and 3)*

It is true that the White Paper does say that size and efficiency do not always go together but in view of the Corporation's subsequent career (when, for example, General Electric and British Leyland, amongst others, were created in their present form), this view seems to have had limited influence.

To obtain at least a partial answer to the question of technical efficiency and size, Prais examined the share of the 100 largest plants (rather than firms) over the period 1930–1968. (This was the longest period for which comparable data were available.) We can reasonably assume that most *technical* economies of scale are exhausted at the *plant* level. But some further production economies may depend on a vertically integrated firm having, say, two manufacturing plants that can achieve long production runs of different products, with both plants being supplied with their materials from one large plant earlier in the production process. In practice the number of cases where genuine *production* economies of vertical integration arise seem to be rare.

If technical economies of scale were of great importance in the growth of the largest firms, we would expect a sizeable increase in the share of the 100 largest plants over this period. In fact, allowing for some margin of error due to changes in the statistical coverage, there was little or no change in the percentage of manufacturing output accounted for by the 100 largest plants: the share varied between 9 and 11% over the whole period. (This does not, of course, mean that the absolute size of the largest 100 plants has not increased. In fact, for manufacturing industry as a whole the median plant size more than doubled from 230 in 1980 to 480 in 1968.[3]) Thus if *firms* had changed in size only to the same extent as *plants*, then the share of the 100 largest firms in net output would have remained at about 20%.

Technical efficiency, therefore, seems to have played little or no part in the growth of aggregate concentration.

It may be suggested, however, that these highly aggregated figures obscure the fact that for many industries very large plant sizes must be used to achieve all available technical economies. It is probably true, for example, that in parts of the chemicals, metal manufacture, shipbuilding, vehicles and aerospace industries, plants employing 1,000 or more are required for efficiency. But there are certainly many other sections of manufacturing industry where technical efficiency requires much smaller plant sizes. In this connection some more recent work by Prais is directly relevant. He compares the median size of plant for 33 comparable manufacturing industries in the UK, Germany and US. For the sample as a whole the median plant size for the US is 370 employees, for Germany 410 and for the UK 440 employees. But in all three countries in one third of the industries the median plant size was 200 employees or less.[4] Clearly it is very unlikely that in all of these industries there is a unique optimum plant size. It is much more likely, for example, that for a considerable range both below and above the median size there is no appreciable increase in production costs. Consequently, we may conclude that there is still enormous scope for plants, even in manufacturing, which employ fewer than 200 people.

Furthermore, there are a number of signs that perhaps firms may have to look much more closely in future at production plans which imply the organisation of very large plants. Engineers may argue that efficient production requires large plant but top management will have to be sure that output and sales targets can actually be achieved. In other words, there is a great deal more to production than large pieces of capital equipment with enormous designed output capacity per time period. This idea was neatly summarised by Stigler as follows: 'Survival is the only test of a firm's ability to cope with all the problems: buying inputs, soothing labourers, finding customers, introducing new products and techniques, coping with fluctuations, evading regulations, etc. A cross-section study of the costs of inputs, per unit of output in a given period, measures only one facet of the firm's efficiency and yields no conclusion on efficiency in the large'.[5]

Fifty years ago this problem was brought home to the Ford Motor Company which had designed the massive River Rouge site, not only to assemble and manufacture parts and components, but also to produce basic materials and supplies. 'By the mid-1920s River Rouge employed 75,000 workers producing coke, pig iron, steel castings, forgings, and parts and components for cars and tractors, as well as carrying on the final assembly'.[6] Even before it was finished it was realised that the whole operation was misconceived. Top management was out of touch with those closer to the production shops and many there felt completely overwhelmed by the sheer size of the operations they were meant to direct and control. Subsequently, much of the complex was closed and the whole trend of operations in the industry was away from centralisation towards a pattern of dispersed assembly plants. Blair suggested, however, that somewhat similar mistakes of over-centralisation may have been repeated in the petrochemical industry, where massive plants have been built using highly specialised equipment which means that breakdowns are extremely costly, because the plant then has to remain idle.

The petro-chemical industry is highly capital intensive but a question of increasing interest in large *labour* intensive plants is the apparent close relationship between plant size and propensity to strike. According to recent evidence from the Department of Employment, for example, only one per cent of manufacturing plants with 25–90 employees suffered a strike in the period 1971–3 but the proportion rose steadily to reach 44% for plants with over 2,000 employees (and even higher for the largest plants)[7]. Not surprisingly 'soothing labourers' proves much more difficult in large impersonal plants than in smaller plants where there is a much closer association between those making a decision and those affected by it on the shop floor.

We may note in passing that this difficulty is only one aspect of the complex phenomenon rechristened by Leibenstein as X-inefficiency. Although the sub-optimising behaviour that he has in mind does not necessarily occur only in large plants and organisations, most of the examples that he gives seem to be bound up with large size interacting with an absence of competitive pressures. Reliable estimates of the extent of losses (through higher costs) resulting from X-inefficiency are still largely lacking but what evidence there is suggests that they may be substantial and on a priori grounds they are likely to be considerably more important than, say, the social loss from monopoly.

Up to this point, then, we have argued that very little of the sharp increase in aggregate concentration can be explained by the demands of large-scale production techniques, at least insofar as these govern plant sizes. Plants in the UK tend to be rather larger on average than either Germany or the USA but it was clear from all three countries that there was still great scope for efficient small-scale production across a range of industries.

If large-scale production methods do not explain the size of the largest firms there must be other factors at work. The conventional view is that there are certain economies of size quite apart from those in production which accrue to the multi-plant *firm* (rather than the single plant). In his recent study Prais examined in some detail the influence of transport and communications, advertising and finance on the generation of massive firm size. For the first two (transport and communications, and advertising) his conclusion was that they had an important and discernible influence on the growth of the large multi-plant firm but that this influence was not a dominant one. Far more important, in his view, were financial factors some of which were largely institutional and perhaps unique to the UK, but there are other features which are of more general applicability. The period since the war has seen a remarkable growth in financial institutions (like pension funds, insurance and investment companies) which by 1972 held more than 40% of all quoted UK ordinary shares and seem likely very soon to hold the greater part of all share capital of quoted industrial companies. These institutions not only have a preference for companies with shares quoted on a Stock Exchange but tend to channel their funds towards the largest of them. In addition the availability for a long period of very cheap debenture finance and certain tax idiosyncrasies have in their turn favoured widespread acquisition. There has thus been a general bias in the market towards very large firms which have found it desirable to use their funds to acquire other companies. Another aspect of this situation is the increasing vulnerability of managements owning only very small fractions of the equity, to a takeover bid. The process of acquisition may then become 'cumulatively reinforcing': a larger size of company leading to smaller director share ownership, giving greater precariousness of control, leading to takeovers which produces even larger companies, and so on.

If there were genuine social economies in this result they would at least partly offset the anxieties aroused by the growth of the largest companies. But here again the social as opposed to the private gains may be limited or even non-existent. Two points can be mentioned, both concerning aspects of risk-taking and both linking up directly with diversification by large enterprises, which we discuss in the next section. Perhaps the most frequent claim made for the benefits of very large *firms* is that by spreading their activities across industries they are able to minimise risks (by reducing profit variability) and therefore the bias in favour of large units is only to be expected and in fact should be encouraged. It is certainly true that up to a point a diversified group does benefit from merging a number of different activities and this provides some incentive for acquisitions. But what is not usually shown is the comparatively small size at which this factor ceases to have any pronounced effect. On the basis of the available evidence from the US and the UK, Prais concluded that this influence probably ceases beyond the quite modest size of 1,000 employees and can therefore have played little part in the growth of the largest enterprises which are fifty times as large.

Furthermore we should remember that none of the risks involved in the different lines of production are altered simply by bringing a number of them under one managerial roof. As Prais puts it: 'The total social product is unaffected by how units are grouped for book-keeping purposes; in other words, the inherent risks and uncertainty of the production process are not escaped merely by combining accounting units into ever-larger groups'[8]. Thus although financial factors have undoubtedly played an important part in the growth of the largest firms and aggregate concentration we should remain sceptical of the social benefits that they bring.

The influences mentioned so far which have worked to a greater or lesser extent in favour of the rapid growth of very large firms (production economies of scale, transport and communications, advertising and finance) may be termed systematic: technical and institutional factors favouring large size. Prais estimated that these may have accounted for one half of the growth in aggregate concentration in the UK since 1950. The remainder he attributed to the process aptly christened 'spontaneous drift'. The general principles of this process are well known.

If all firms have the same chance of equal proportionate growth in any time period but growth rates are subject to some variability (ie some firms actually grow at a fast rate while others grow slowly or decline) then over time a highly skewed (or concentrated) distribution of firms will emerge. The greater the variability in growth rates the faster the unequal distribution is generated. Thus if chance factors *alone* operate on the size distribution of firms, concentration would increase without limit. In practice, of course, systematic factors are also at work and these may outweigh, balance or reinforce the chance factors. Important diseconomies of scale and an aggressive antitrust policy, for example, could outweigh the tendency for increased concentration. According to Prais' analysis, in the first half of this century in the UK there were no strong systematic factors favouring the faster growth of larger firms over smaller and consequently aggregate concentration rose only slowly as a result of 'spontaneous drift'. In fact it is possible that the controls over the allocation of materials imposed during and immediately after the Second World War may have worked in favour of medium and small firms and hence stabilised the level of concentration. Since the early 1950s systematic factors, especially those to do with finance mentioned above, have caused a dramatic shift in favour of large companies. Consequently for the last twenty-five years or so Britain has experienced a very rapid increase in concentration with the chance factors reinforced by systematic factors.

Now if roughly half of the concentration increase can be attributed to 'spontaneous drift' and an important part of the remainder has been due to financial factors which may have little or no social (as opposed to private) advantage we may seriously question whether the whole process of concentration has produced much net benefit. Furthermore, as discussed in the next section, one aspect of the concentration increase may have serious long term effects on the performance of industry. If the benefits of increased concentration have been slight (and possibly negative) then policies which aim to reverse the trend may not cause the large social losses that are sometimes claimed.

III Diversification and competition

The rapid growth of the largest companies, to an important extent through a large increase in the number of plants operated by each company, has produced in the UK the simultaneous occurrence of a high level of aggregate concentration and diversification. By 1974 just under one quarter of all employment in the largest 200 manufacturing firms was in industries outside what may be regarded as their base technology; more precisely in industries outside the industrial order to which they had been classified and where the greater part of their activity was concentrated. On average they operated in ten separate industries each and members of the group operated in every one of the 120 industries into which the manufacturing sector is divided for statistical purposes. The scope and diversity of their activities means, of course, that they are likely to encounter each other in many different industries where they have varying market shares. A frequent occurrence may be that one of the market leaders is also one of the largest firms overall (in the manufacturing sector) but in addition several other very large firms may also participate in the industry but with relatively modest market shares. One estimate, for example, suggests that in about half of all manufacturing industries the largest firms overall are also amongst the three market leaders and on average a further five of the largest firms will be active in the industry.[9]

In the ten industries singled out by Prais as showing substantial declines in the number of small establishments (with ten employees or fewer) over the period 1935-1968 the employment share of the largest 200 enterprises averaged 30% by 1974 and they were operating an average of 79 establishments. Whereas the largest firms appear to be encroaching on territory previously occupied almost exclusively by small firms (like branches of the food, clothing, textiles, timber and furniture industries) the average size of their plants has so far remained well below that of the average for the industry as a whole. As yet, therefore, there can be little in the way of production economies of scale to account for the development.

As the phenomenon is a relatively new one there are no very settled conclusions about the likely effects, especially the long run effects on industrial structure and performance. Perhaps the most widely quoted discussions of this issue are those of Blair[10] and Edwards[11]. They have placed particular emphasis on the deep pocket hypothesis and latterly on the spread of 'mutual forbearance' in the competitive behaviour of the largest firms as they encounter each other in many markets. If correct, both views are likely to have serious consequences for medium and small firms. Briefly the 'deep pocket' hypothesis suggests that large firms operating across a wide spectrum of different industries will earn in some of them high profits because of their market power. They will thus be able to use these profits as an instrument for increasing their market shares in industries which they wish to enter. In particular they will be able to subsidise losses in these industries while they are charging uneconomic prices aimed at eliminating or coercing smaller and more specialised rivals. This tactic cannot be used by the existing firms since they are unlikely to have the resources in the form of high profits earned elsewhere with which to subsidise price cuts. Once the tactic has been successful, on this view, the large diversifying firm will be able to recoup its previous loss by raising prices. The main sufferers from such a policy would initially be smaller, more specialised firms and then consumers of the product.

On a number of grounds both theoretical and empirical, we do not find this line of argument very convincing. For example unless the diversifying firm can be sure that other firms (including other large firms) will not enter the industry once it raises its prices it will have to face renewed competition. If the industry concerned was previously a competitive one, with many firms, entry is likely to be relatively easy (and incidentally, returns near average for manufacturing). If on the other hand, the industry was previously oligopolistic and earning relatively high returns making it more attractive to the diversifier, then existing firms are likely to be able to withstand a period of price competition. Indeed in this case it may be the diversifying firm, fresh to the industry, which is at a disadvantage.

The direct empirical evidence on this issue is sparse. Most authorities have relied on past antitrust cases which on closer examination deal usually with the actions of an entrenched monopolist defending its position from an energetic entrant rather than with those of a large diversifying firm trying to establish its position in a new market. A recent review of a number of Monopolies Commission reports in the UK tends to confirm this view, ie that predatory pricing does take place – there have been some notorious examples – but it is an instrument used by established monopolists not by diversifying firms[12].

The second hypothesis, concerned with 'mutual forbearance', seems a much more insidious and therefore potentially more dangerous result of high concentration coupled with widespread diversification. The process has been described by Edwards as follows:

'The multiplicity of their (large diversified firms') contacts may blunt the edge of their competition. A prospect of advantage from vigorous competition in one market may be weighed against the danger of retaliatory forays by the competitor in other markets. Each conglomerate competitor may adopt a live-and-let-live policy designed to stabilise the whole structure of the competitive relationship ... Like national states, the great conglomerates may come to have recognised spheres of influence and may hesitate to fight local wars vigorously because the prospects of local gain are not worth the risk of general warfare'.[13]

As mentioned briefly above there is already evidence that the largest companies in manufacturing in the UK encounter each other's subsidiaries in a great number of industries as a result of the extraordinarily rapid growth in the number of separate plants they operate. Whether this structure has yet led to the kind of behaviour suggested by Edwards is more difficult to establish. There is some tentative evidence that 'entry' by large diversifying firms to industries apparently remote from their previous experience may be associated with lower profit margins.[14] But the conventional view of this result would be that new competition, whether from small or large firms, was having the desired effect and improving the allocative performance of industry. Far from having the dire consequences that some commentators have suggested diversification may actually have a salutary procompetitive effect.

In the longer term this interpretation may be too optimistic. The results mentioned refer to 1972, following the period of unprecedented concentration change. It is therefore possible that the full consolidation of any gains from this growth had still to be made. In individual industries the realignment of market shares may have still been taking place and this was reflected in lower profitability. Once the concentration increase slackens, then presumably firms will be seeking to consolidate their position and if necessary to reach some form of tacit agreement with their major rivals. At this stage prices and profitability might be expected to rise and the kind of behaviour envisaged by Edwards come into force. In their primary industries the largest companies are used to the tacit collusion familiar in oligopoly: what more natural than that they should reach a similar accommodation in those secondary industries into which they have diversified? The growth of aggregate concentration may thus hasten the spread of oligopolistic behaviour even where some of the market shares of the largest companies are modest, in accordance with acknowledged 'spheres of influence'. The process may be insidious precisely because it does not involve any violent and direct action (like predatory pricing) against smaller rivals which may bring an antitrust action against an offender. Instead it may ensure that the scope for individual initiatives by medium and small firms is continually restricted, not through any discriminatory policies by the largest companies but simply because the prospects for smaller companies of successfully entering industries not only dominated by market leaders which are amongst the country's largest companies but also where a number of subsidiaries of other massive companies are active. In this way entry to different industries may pass largely into the hands of a relatively small group of giants through their diversifying activities and instead of being one of the sharpest instruments for regulating industrial performance, entry may thus turn into one of the dullest. The prospect may then be one of an increasingly inflexible and sluggish industrial sector with greatly diminished opportunities for smaller firms.

It is as well to remember Marshall's warning about the spread of monopoly, which is equally appropriate in the present context: 'the prima facie arguments in favour of the fusion of monopolistic cartels, or other associations, in complementary branches of industry, though often plausible and even strong, will generally be found on closer examination to be treacherous. They point to the removal of prominent social and industrial discords; but at the probable expense of larger and more enduring discords in the future'.[15]

IV Conclusions

We have argued in this chapter that the economic case for the massive size of the largest UK companies is much less firmly based than is frequently claimed. In particular their rapid growth in the last 30 years owes much to factors, like 'spontaneous drift' and biases in the capital market, that bring little productive benefit. It also appeared that where the concentration increase had proceeded furthest (in the UK) the position of small firms had been curtailed far more than in similar advanced industrial economies (like Germany,

France and the USA).

We suggested, in addition, that continued diversification by the largest companies may involve the subtle danger of further unintentional restrictions on the entry by small and medium sized firms into many areas of the manufacturing sector dominated by the largest companies and their subsidiaries.

It might be thought that the spectacular concentration increase in the UK could be reversed by similarly dramatic policy measures. But really drastic action, like the partition of the largest companies into a number of roughly equal rivals, is neither feasible nor desirable. The USA which has in the past employed this measure has been very reluctant to use it recently on any scale.

One suggestion that could be more fully explored was made by Prais at the end of his recent study. We have noted the special emphasis he placed on financial factors in his analysis of the rapid growth of the largest companies, especially the bias that the capital market now has for large firms. It was also apparent that while companies had found it advantageous to acquire others, there were actually strong disincentives for them to divest themselves of unprofitable subsidiaries. Thus a company wishing to hive off some of its subsidiaries and to reimburse shareholders by new shares in the separate parts was inhibited by the tax laws. The new shares would probably have been treated as distributions subject to income tax and surtax. To help offset the bias while leaving decisions in the hands of the companies themselves, Prais suggests the possibility of a progressive corporation tax which could be adjusted to yield the same amount as the present tax and if necessary to give relief to those (few) firms where production methods require really large plants (employing, say, more than 10,000 people). Simultaneously this would provide firms with an incentive to monitor closely the performance of their subsidiaries and thus balance returns (net of tax) from their operation against their sale value and the reduced tax liability that might result.

A rather similar proposal would aim to reduce the incentive for some companies to undertake such heavy advertising in markets where even the private return may be very low but where the cumulative effect on new entry may be important. If advertising expenditures above certain limits were made non-deductible for tax purposes this too would eventually help to redress the balance in favour of smaller firms.

In addition to these kinds of discriminatory tax provisions there is scope, certainly in the UK, for a much tougher approach to antitrust policy. It is significant that in the country where antitrust is probably most severe – the USA – aggregate concentration has remained roughly stable for more than 20 years. It is also symptomatic of the half-hearted approach in the UK that the Monopolies and Mergers Commission has uncovered a number of secret agreements which should have been registered under the law but which were not. At present no action can be taken against either the companies or their managers for thus disobeying the law.

The most direct method of rapid growth is by merger and there is a large gulf between UK merger controls and those applied under the US antitrust laws. Prais mentions that about one-third of the recent growth of the largest British companies may be attributed to mergers, whereas for the US the figure is more like one-tenth. Much tighter controls, therefore, over acquisitions by the largest companies might make a similar contribution to halting the growth of concentration in the UK. The objection that any form of blanket prohibition lacks rationality since many mergers may yield net benefits, can be met by pointing to the growing body of evidence that shows, on the contrary, the unhappiness of many such marriages.[16]

Finally, the recent experience in the UK with state sponsored organisations for assisting (and restructuring) industry has been ambiguous. At times they have tended to use their influence and resources to reinforce rather than counterbalance concentration growth. At the time of the IRC, there were a number of occasions when it seemed to be working in opposition to a body like the Monopolies and Mergers Commission. If reasonable policies are to prevail it is essential that such organisations should keep their munificence for medium-sized and small firms.

References

1. This chapter draws on two studies completed at the National Institute of Economic and Social Research in London: *The evolution of giant firms in Britain*, by S. J. Prais, CUP, revised edition 1981, and *Diversification and competition*, by M. A. Utton, CUP, 1979.
2. Prais, S. J., *op. cit.*
3. *Ibid.*
4. Prais, S. J., *Productivity and industrial structure*, CUP, 1981.
5. Stigler, G. J., 'Monopoly and oligopoly by merger', reprinted in *The organisation of industry*, Irvin, 1968.
6. Blair, J. M., *Economic concentration*, Harcourt, Brace, Jovanovich, 1972.
7. Prais, S. J., 'The strike proneness of large plants in Britain', *Journal of the Royal Statistical Society*, series A, vol 141, 1978.
8. Prais, S. J., *The evolution of giant firms in Britain, op. cit.*
9. Utton, M. A., *op. cit.*
10. Blair, J. M., *op. cit.*
11. Edwards, C. D., in *Hearings before the Sub-Committee on Antitrust and Monopoly of the Committee of the Judiciary of The United States Senate, Part I: overall and conglomerate aspects*, Washington, 1964.
12. Utton, M. A., *op. cit.*
13. Edwards, *op. cit.*
14. Utton, *op. cit.*
15. Marshall, A., *Principles of economics*, 8th edition, Macmillan, 1924 (reprinted 1961).
16. Meeks, G., *Disappointing marriage: a study of the gains from merger*, CUP, 1977.

CHAPTER 2

An analysis of concentration

J. M. Samuels and P. A. Morrish

This chapter brings together pertinent findings of a number of researchers, and aims to provide material which can be used as a basis for further discussion on the role of small business. Some of the studies quoted are historical and refer to what was happening in the 1960s; that was a time when small firms were neglected. If more notice of their problems had been taken then, we would be in a better position today.

I Aggregate concentration

Since the end of the Second World War there has been a rise in concentration in most countries. In many countries governments have actively encouraged this, in attempts to 'rationalise' their industrial structures. In France in the 1950s and 1960s, there was a fear that the size of their companies put them at a competitive disadvantage with their main trading rivals. As late as 1972, the French stock exchanges were trying to stimulate interest in mergers and takeovers.

In the UK the 'urge to merge' of the late 1960s and early 1970s was partly the result of government action. The Industrial Reorganisation Corporation was attempting to prepare the UK economy for entry into the EEC. It was doing this by encouraging the development of larger units, at a time when the UK already had more giant enterprises than the other member countries of the EEC.

Were all these attempts to encourage industry to organise into large-scale units a mistake? Is it correct to believe that in order to compete successfully in the international market place, one needs to be a large enterprise? Much has been written about economies of scale, not all of which is supported by evidence; but undoubtedly there are economies of scale, and one such area where they do apply is in the provision of finance.[1]

Table 1 shows that the rise in concentration in the UK since 1949 has been at a fairly steady rate. At the end of the 1970s, approximately half of all manufacturing output in the UK was produced by the hundred largest enterprises in the country. If the trend continues, then by the year 2000 the 100 largest firms will be responsible for approximately 90% of manufacturing net output. The question that has not been answered is, do the disadvantages from being organised into large units outweigh the economies that come about from being large?

It should be appreciated that even if mergers and takeovers had not been encouraged, concentration would have increased in most countries. Gibrat's law states that if firms of all sizes have the same probability of growth, that is if large and small firms have the same chance of doubling their size, this will still lead to an increase over time in the degree of concentration. Of course, if economies of scale do exist, large firms will have the greater opportunity to grow at a given rate, leading to yet faster increases in concentration.

What has happened over the last two decades is that it has become increasingly difficult to set up new firms and the merger takeover process has worked in favour of the large firms. The probability of being taken over decreases as the size of firm increases, as does the probability of liquidation. These processes, coupled with Gibrat's law, mean that concentration has increased, and will continue to increase, irrespective of economies of scale. That is, concentration will increase unless something is done to alter the existing tendencies.

In fact there is disagreement as to whether increasing concentration is continuous and inevitable. Hannah and Kay argue that since 1919 mergers have been the dominant force leading to increased concentration in the UK.[2] They argue that the significance of mergers has been increasing, and that they now account for essentially all of the currently observed increase in net concentration. Hart[3] and Prais[4] disagree; they accept that the effect of mergers on concentration since 1960 has been important, but do not accept that the evidence supports the view that mergers were the major reason for the growth of concentration. A tough anti-merger policy might slow up the increase in concentration, but would not stop it. All four researchers do agree that mergers of large concerns need public supervision and constraint.

One alarming feature of this trend is not just the concentration of production into a few hands, but also the fact that many of the largest 100 companies are multinational businesses with their headquarters, their home base, outside the United Kingdom. However, before the nationalist flag is waved it should be appreciated that the UK is the second largest home country for multinationals. Britain is still a net creditor, and owns substantially more assets in foreign countries than foreigners own in the UK.

II Industry concentration

Some industries need very large scale of investment before they can operate at an efficient level. Just to consider aggregate concentration ratios can be misleading. A country may have comparative advantages in industries that have to be large scale and so must show higher aggregate concentration figures than a country that specialises in industries that do not need large investment and plant.

We will now consider two issues: first, the variation in concentration between industries within a country, and second, the differences between countries in the concentration ratios for a particular industry.

Table 2 shows the range of five-firm concentration ratios for a number of product groups in the UK in 1968, ie the extent to which the five largest firms dominate an industry. As can be seen, 83 of the 340 product groups have a concentration ratio in excess of 90%. Table 3 names certain product groups, and enables us to compare four-firm concentration ratios for a particular industry across countries. The figures relate to the year 1963. The industries are listed in an order depending upon the firm concentration ratios in the UK. In a UK/West German comparison, it is not until one gets down to electronic apparatus, with a 33% ratio in the UK, that West Germany shows a higher level of concentration. Even then it is only in a few industries that West Germany shows higher concentration than in the UK.

What is more surprising is the distribution of four-plant concentration ratios (also shown in Table 3). There are now many cases in key growth and export industries where West Germany shows higher plant concentration than the UK. This suggests that the industrial structure of the UK tends to be organised on the basis of a few large firms with many comparatively small plants, whereas West Germany has fewer large firms but each one operating larger-scale plant than in the UK. It would suggest the UK has been looking for firm economies of scale and West Germany for plant economies of scale. France seems to follow the West German pattern. It should be emphasised that these figures relate to 1963 and there has been a great deal of growth and merger and takeover activities in these countries since that year.

III Relative importance of manufacturing industries

Table 3 displays the concentration ratios by industry for three countries. However, some industries are clearly more important than others; for example, the fact that the fur industry in the UK had a four-firm concentration ratio of 21 is of little importance when compared with a ratio of 40 for autos and parts. Table 4 shows the relative importance of manufacturing industry in four countries.

The relative importance of an industry within a country and the size of the companies within that industry, are clearly significant. Some industries need to be organised into larger units than do others. Some industries have growth and export potential, whereas others are declining and are industries which can easily be entered by developing countries. In any move, therefore, to decrease or to increase the levels of concentration, one has to be selective.

The relative importance of each industry in terms of percentage of total output varies country by country, as shown in Table 4. Furthermore, an analysis of the distribution of the largest companies by industry shows a divergence of emphasis between Britain and her major competitors (Table 5).

The largest companies in Britain are in the food, drink and tobacco industries, whereas in Germany the chemical and metal products industries have the largest companies.

One factor which has had a big impact on government policies across countries over many years, has been export performance. Table 6 shows the export performance of manufacturing industries in the UK and West Germany from 1954 to 1972. This indicates that Britain has the largest companies in industries with small export potential – the opposite to West Germany. Furthermore, when one looks at plants (establishments) rather than companies, this feature is further emphasised. Britain has smaller plants compared with West Germany in the important exporting industries, as shown in Table 7.

Admittedly, Table 6 shows actual export performance and this is not the same as export potential. It is possible that the UK, with different policies and organisation, could have performed better than it did in the industries in which it had the smaller firms and smaller establishments. Indeed, the Japanese export boom was based on government encouragement of medium-sized firms. The large Japanese firms which were dominant at home, did not need exports as badly as did the medium-sized firms. The Japanese policy is not to protect the smaller firms' share of the home market but to encourage and help them to sell abroad.

IV Productivity in manufacturing industries

Is it possible to link productivity to size of firms, establishments and/or concentration? The evidence on the relationship between size of employment units and productivity is inconclusive. In a review of eight studies carried out in the USA and Britain, Porter and Lawler found that in only three studies was the productivity of workers employed in small sections higher than that of workers employed in medium- and large-size sections. In three other studies, including the one by Revans (1958) of the British National Coal Board, workers employed in medium-sized sections had significantly higher productivity than workers in large sections. Further to confound matters, two of the studies reviewed by Porter and Lawley (1965) showed that there was no significant relationship between section size and labour productivity.

Table 9 illustrates the well known fact that the growth in output per person employed in the UK has been well below that to be found in other countries. Many explanations have, of course, been offered for this, ranging over restrictive practices, poor management and inadequate investment. Tables 9 and 10 relate to more recent years and again show that the UK compares unfavourably with her competitors in terms of productivity. These two tables show across industry, output/capital ratios for particular countries. Table 11 shows the growth in labour productivity in the UK and West Germany by industry. Taking the whole period, from 1954 to 1972, the growth in labour productivity is higher in West Germany than in the UK, in all the industries.

In order to consider the UK in more detail we analyse in Table 12 and Table 13 output per worker by concentration ratio. It appears that as concentration increases up to a level of approximately 80% (five-firm concentration ratio), the output per worker rises. Higher levels of concentration, perhaps indicating the absence of competition, leads to a fall in productivity. This would lend support to the idea that effective operation requires firms of a certain size and if there is a limit to the size of the market-place one can only have a certain number of firms above this minimum viable size. Therefore, a level of concentration above, say, the 20% range, would be expected to lead to increased output per worker.

A further point for discussion is that West Germany has higher plant concentration than the UK, which means larger units of plant, and therefore has possible economies of scale which could explain the higher productivity to be found in West Germany. Again, the proposition that increased concentration leads to increased productivity is supported.

V   Mergers and takeovers

The contribution of mergers and takeovers to the increase in concentration was discussed in an earlier section. It is well known that in the UK the late 1960s and early 1970s were periods of hectic merger and takeover activity. Each merger or acquisition was accompanied by optimistic statements with regard to the long-term gains to the UK economy, but the Monopolies Commission was, in fact, forced to conclude that the wave of merger activity had an impact on the economy in terms of productivity and growth which was, at best, neutral.

Although United Kingdom companies have been keen to grow through acquisition, the level of investment by UK companies has not been as impressive as that of its European competitors (see Table 14). Table 15 reveals that in the UK the percentage share of the GDP that is invested in the manufacturing sector has been steadily declining over time. We have been relatively neglectful of fiscal investment in the manufacturing sector. One of the reasons for this is the low level of profitability in this sector. To compare profitability across countries is extremely difficult, but Table 16 shows one attempt at such a comparison.

Two decades of a high level of merger and takeover activity in the UK do not appear to have led to improved profitability or to higher levels of investment. Whittington[5], who has undertaken numerous studies of the relationship between size of company and profitability, concludes in a recent paper that,

'With regard to incentives to greater industrial concentration, it is clear that profitability does not, on average, provide an incentive for larger firms to grow at a relatively high rate. Equally, it does not provide them with the means for greater growth, in terms of a high level of profits which might potentially be retained. There does appear to be some reward for size in the form of greater stability of the rate of return through time and in the form of less inter-firm varia- tion of profitability, so that size brings a better prospect that profitability will be adequate.'

Whittington points to an interesting complementary between his own findings and those of other researchers on the subject.

'Singh[6] found that the main characteristic distinguishing taking-over from taken-over firms was their size, so that size can be regarded as a form of protection for management against take-over. Newbould[7] found that strategic motives, such as control over markets and other environmental factors, seemed to dominate in the take-over decision, and Meeks[8] established that the post-merger profitability of companies was disappointing relative to pre-merger profitability. These results taken together suggest that take-overs and mergers are largely initiated to create or maintain large companies with relatively poor profitability but with stable market environments over which they have some control.'

On average, the many mergers and takeovers in the UK, leading to increased industrial concentration, do not appear to have led to higher levels of investment and productivity.

VI   Births and deaths

One factor that has led to an acceleration in the rate of increase in concentration is merger and takeover activity. It is the smaller and medium-sized companies that are exposed to a higher probability of being purchased. It is also the small and medium size that disappear because of liquidation.

Ijiri and Simon (1971) find, on examining the largest 500 companies in the USA, that the survival probability is the same for firms of all sizes. We would agree that the survival probability is the same for companies in the largest size groups, but the survival probability for companies in different size groups is far from similar, the probability of survival increases with company size. Survival is a motivation for a large number of mergers and takeovers; although it is not often discussed by the participants. The defensive merger is discussed in terms of the usual jargon about economies of scale and rationalisation. The results of a study by Chesher and Samuels indicate that over the 1960s the probability of survival did not increase once a company had a capital employed greater than £5 million (in 1960 values).

This result is comparable to that found by Singh (1971) for an earlier period. In examining the period from 1948 to 1960 Singh shows that the probability of survival did not increase with size, once a company had a capital employed greater than £4 million. Allowing for the effects of inflation, it is suggested that these two results are similar, and that the same real size safety barrier has existed over a long period.

Table 17 shows that a clear distinction can be drawn between groups 1 to 5 and groups 6 to 10; the probability of surviving for the decade for the former being in the region of 0.74 and for the latter in the region of 0.50. The probability of takeover is (with the exception of group 6) a decreasing function of size with, very approximately, the smallest companies having twice the probability of being taken over than the largest companies have.

The really dramatic differences in survival probability can be explained in terms of liquidations. During the decade none of the companies sampled in the largest seven size groups were liquidated.

(However, Rolls-Royce was one of the companies sampled in group 2, and it came to its sad end early in the 1970s.) Liquidations did occur in groups 8, 9 and 10 at a rate which decreased with size.

The survival probabilities of companies in the smallest group are surprisingly small. For those quoted companies with a capital employed of less than £250,000 in 1960, the estimated probability of surviving until the end of 1969 was only 0.41, an estimated 42% of such companies were taken over and 17% went into liquidation.

These figures can be compared with the survival probabilities for small, non-quoted companies given in the Bolton Report and shown in Table 18.

The definition of a small firm used in the Bolton study was a firm employing 200 or less people. As explained, such firms are usually too small to be quoted on the Stock Exchange and are, in most cases, much smaller than the smallest companies in our sample. It can be seen that the probability of these small firms being taken over is, for each industry group, considerably less than for the small quoted companies. However, the table in the Bolton Report gives estimates of the probability of being taken over during an eight-year period, whereas Table 17 refers to a ten-year period; but even when the Bolton figures are standardised for a ten-year period they still show a much lower probability.

One reason why this probability of death as a result of takeover is greater for small quoted companies than for small, non-quoted companies, is because a company with shares quoted on the market is easier to acquire. It is sometimes suggested that one reason why certain companies seek a market quotation is so that they can make themselves an easier target for takeover. One result, however, that has emerged from our study of new companies, is that they do not have a higher probability of being taken over than companies that already have a quotation.

With regard to death through liquidation, the results for the two types of small companies are not so different. The Bolton Committee's small firms showed (adjusted to ten years) a 10% chance of being liquidated in the manufacturing and the construction and motor trade groups and a 24% and 19% chance in the wholesale and the retail groups respectively. The small group in the Samuels Chesher sample (group 10) consisted of a mixture of companies from many industries including wholesaling and retailing; so the finding of a 17% chance of being liquidated at some point over a ten-year period for this heterogeneous group is not different to the finding for the small (under 200 employees) category described in the Bolton Report.

VII   Reduction in the number of companies with a market quotation

That concentration is increasing in industry is well known. The stock market, or rather those who operate through the market, must accept much of the responsibility for this state of affairs. The investment policies of the large institutions have led to an increase in the proportion of the nation's savings being invested in the largest companies. The market has allowed businessmen to play their takeover games and has, perhaps, actively encouraged this type of development. As Caves (1968) pointed out, a much larger proportion of the growth in US industry can be accounted for by internal expansion than could the growth of UK industry. When a British industrialist wants to expand, his typical reaction is to buy up another company.

The stock market itself needs to become worried, for the number of deaths of quoted companies is vastly exceeding the number of births. There are fewer companies available in which the investor can buy an equity interest. The serious situation can be seen in the reduction in the number of companies with a quotation on the London Stock Exchange. The number of firms with a quotation in the market was about the same in 1960 as in 1948. However, as Singh (1971) has pointed out over the latter part of this period, from 1954 to 1960, the number of deaths greatly exceeded the number of births; the incidence of deaths being double the incidence of births. Singh shows that the death rate over this period was unprecedented in any other observed period. He found that takeover only became the predominant cause of death for quoted companies during the 1950s. Prior to that, as Hart and Prais have shown, liquidation was the most common cause.

VIII   Conclusion

If it is thought necessary to encourage small and medium-size firms, a major change in policy needs to be made. The market forces have been working against them for at least 30 years. To neglect them is not in the interests of the UK. The emphasis on bigness has not brought about the hoped-for improvement in the competitiveness of the UK economy. Despite the Bolton Committee Report, the Wilson Committee Report and the electioneering statements of the Conservative Party in 1979, the position of the small firm has not improved. Industrial concentration has continued to increase with few obvious signs of improvements in our relative economic position. It is to be hoped that the further statements promising help for the smaller firm made during the 1983 election will lead to action, and a real revival in that sector of the economy.

TABLE 1

Shares of the hundred largest enterprises and establishments in manufacturing net output, United Kingdom.

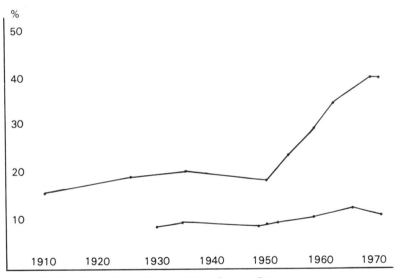

SOURCE: S. J. Prais, *The Evolution of Giant Firms in Britain.*

TABLE 2

Seller Concentration in Selected UK Markets, 1968[1]

Concentration class[2] (range of five-firm concentration ratio %)	Number of product groups in class	%
0–9	0	0.0
10–19	8	2.4
20–29	20	5.9
30–39	28	8.2
40–49	34	10.0
50–59	47	13.8
60–69	36	10.6
70–79	38	11.2
80–89	46	13.5
90–100	83	24.4
TOTAL	340	100.0

1. The markets included are sub-minimum list heading product groups in mining and quarrying and manufacturing, for which five-firm concentration ratios are available.

2. The meaning of this column is that there are no product groups in which the largest five firms account for less than 10% of total sales, eight in which they account for 10–19%, and so on.

SOURCE: A. R. Prest and D. J. Coppock, *The U.K. Economy: A Manual of Applied Economics.*

TABLE 3

Four-firm and four-plant concentration ratios, UK, Germany and France, 1963, by Industry Group

	4-firm concentration ratio			4-plant concentration ratio			4-firm / 4-plant		
	UK	WG	France	UK	WG	France	UK	WG	France
Sugar	95	41	42	42	15	22	2.22	2.82	2.10
Tobacco	88	34	100	33	13	18	2.45	2.86	–
Watches and clocks	66	29	24	46	23	20	1.37	1.31	1.19
Aircraft	65	59	57	18	42	20	3.65	1.48	2.65
Motor cycles	65	25	43	45	21	27	1.47	1.20	1.48
Alcohol	58	13	13	31	11	9	1.75	1.21	1.51
Office Machinery	54	53	67	31	35	43	1.71	1.57	1.69
Grain Milling	51	10	10	16	9	7	3.10	1.20	1.44
Bread, biscuits	48	4	15	6	3	10	8.20	1.21	1.42
Glass	48	21	39	18	14	15	2.63	1.34	2.64
Confectionery	47	25	15	32	19	12	1.47	1.33	1.20
Textile machinery	45	28	23	25	24	23	1.76	1.20	1.05
General chemicals	44	38	35	13	33	11	3.43	1.30	3.05
Beer and malt	41	7	24	9	5	15	4.46	1.31	1.67
Domestic elect. app.	40	28	25	27	21	16	1.51	1.18	1.42
Autos and parts	40	39	50	16	28	38	2.56	1.36	1.42
Soft drinks	40	15	22	14	–	9	3.00	–	2.99
Games, toys	38	18	11	17	16	9	2.13	1.14	1.24
Canned frozen food	35	12	15	15	8	9	2.37	1.37	1.91
Paper and board	35	25	26	11	11	12	3.11	2.40	2.25
Rubber and asbestos	35	34	50	18	31	32	1.95	1.14	1.55
Electronic apparatus	33	37	43	11	13	11	3.11	3.05	4.34
Jewellery, etc.	27	11	9	12	8	8	2.23	1.33	1.14

Textile finishing	24	15	37	6	13	15	4.29	1.11	2.32
Metal working tools	22	8	13	11	8	7	2.09	1.00	1.85
Scientific instruments	21	17	22	11	15	18	1.89	1.08	1.23
Mattresses and bedding	21	18	25	10	13	14	1.88	1.39	1.79
Fur	21	8	15	16	8	8	1.15	1.01	1.28
Paper and board products	17	12	5	7	5	4	2.19	2.17	1.20
Wool	16	14	14	5	–	13	2.86	–	1.09
Footwear	16	19	13	6	11	7	2.35	1.75	1.95
Hosiery	16	10	7	5	4	5	3.02	2.32	1.41
Printing and publishing	16	6	7	5	5	5	3.18	1.26	1.43
Mining machinery	15	21	14	12	14	8	1.26	1.36	1.72
Wood furniture	15	4	3	6	3	2	2.55	1.21	1.34
Clay and pottery	13	18	14	6	–	7	2.18	–	1.98
Leather and tanning	12	39	16	6	34	11	1.86	1.19	1.47
Leather products	12	5	6	9	5	5	1.40	1.06	1.18
Plastic	11	10	6	6	7	6	1.99	1.35	1.00
Clothing	9	4	2	3	1	1	3.33	3.21	1.93
Timber	6	4	3	4	2	1	1.35	2.52	2.32

SOURCE: M. Panic, *The U.K. and West German Manufacturing Industry, 1954–72.*

TABLE 4

Relative Importance of Manufacturing Industries, in Selected European Countries, 1970[1]

	Percentage of manufacturing output			
	UK	France	West Germany	Italy
Food, drink and tobacco	11.24	–	10.37	11.80
Chemicals	8.72	28.04	18.12	13.45
Basic Metals	7.68	15.16	8.08	7.06
Iron and steel	5.73	12.17	6.77	5.84
Non-ferrous metals	1.95	2.98	1.31	1.21
Metal Products	42.78	23.51	41.38	31.53
Non-electrical machinery	13.42	–	11.46	11.58
Transport equipment	11.81	9.43	8.52	7.94
Textiles, clothing, leather	10.21	12.17	7.86	16.98
Other manufacturing	19.38	21.12	14.19	19.18
All manufacturing	100.00	100.00	100.00	100.00
Manufacturing Output in thousand millions of I.U.A.[2]	34.3	49.9	79.2	23.9

SOURCES: Industrial Production: Quarterly Supplement to Main Economic Indicators of 4th Quarter, 1975, OECD, and General Statistics 1975, Statistics Office of the European Commission.

1.   The figures have been extracted from tables containing weights for mining.

2.   International Units of Account are an E.E.C. monetary unit based on the gold content of the US dollar prior to its devaluation in December, 1971.

[*SOURCE*: Prest and Coppock.]

TABLE 5

Industrial composition of the 150 largest EEC companies, 1971

Industry sector	Total	UK	WG	Fr'ce	Italy	Neth.	Belg.	Lux.
Food, drink, tobacco	24	20½	1	2	–	½	–	–
Textiles	4	3	–	1	–	–	–	–
Paper and printing	4	3	–	1	–	–	–	–
Building materials	7	5	–	2	–	–	–	–
Rubber	3	½	1	1	½	–	–	–
Mining	9	4	2	3	–	–	–	–
Vehicles, aircraft	14	4	4	5	1	–	–	–
Electrical engineering	16	7	5	2	1	1	–	–
Oil	8	2½	1	2	1	½	1	–
Chemicals	23	4	9½	4	2	2	1½	–
Metals, metal products	36	8	17	5	1	2	2	1
Other	2	–	1	–	1	–	–	–
Total	150	61½	41½	28	7½	6	4½	1

Industrial Composition of the 150 largest EEC companies, 1976

	Total	UK	WG	Fr'ce	Italy	Neth.	Belg.	Lux.
Food, drink, tobacco	22	18½	1	2	–	½	–	–
Textiles	3	2	–	–	1	–	–	–
Paper and printing	4	1	2	1	–	–	–	–
Building materials	6	4	–	2	–	–	–	–
Rubber	2	½	–	1	½	–	–	–
Mining	7	3	2	2	–	–	–	–
Vehicles, aircraft	17	7	4	4	2	–	–	–
Electrical engineering	14	5	6	2	–	1	–	–
Oil	23	5½	5	4	4	1½	3	–
Chemicals	16	2	7	3	1	2	1	–
Metal, metal products	22	3	11	3	1	1	2	1
Other	14	5	4	4	1	–	–	–
Total	150	56½	42	28	10½	6	6	1

TABLE 6

Export ratios by manufacturing industries, UK and West Germany, 1954-72, percentages based on current values (ranking in brackets)

Industry	1954 UK	1954 WG	1959 UK	1959 WG	1963 UK	1963 WG	1968 UK	1968 WG	1972 UK	1972 WG	Average UK	Average WG
Vehicles and aircraft	25.0	24.8	33.0	33.2	26.5	35.7	29.6	47.9	24.7	46.0	27.8 (1)	37.5 (2)
Engineering and electrical goods	22.7	29.2	19.1	30.3	22.4	31.7	21.8	39.6	25.2	37.1	22.2 (2)	33.6 (3)
Chemicals and allied industries	19.4	20.3	17.9	20.9	18.0	21.2	18.5	25.7	20.3	27.0	18.8 (3)	23.0 (4)
Shipbuilding and marine engineering	16.4	30.0	20.9	40.7	12.7	40.0	19.8	39.5	20.8	55.1	18.1 (4)	41.0 (1)
Textiles	15.0	9.5	16.3	9.6	16.3	11.5	15.0	16.3	18.3	20.7	16.2 (5)	13.5 (8)
Other manufacturing	15.8	21.2	12.2	18.1	13.2	16.5	12.6	23.9	13.4	24.1	13.4 (6)	20.7 (6)
Metal manufacturing	12.5	12.9	10.8	18.1	11.7	17.4	12.7	24.3	14.5	20.5	12.4 (7)	18.6 (7)
Metal goods n.e.s.	10.6	21.1	14.5	23.0	9.8	17.1	13.8	23.4	9.5	23.4	11.6 (8)	21.6 (5)
Bricks, pottery, glass and cement	13.3	10.9	10.5	10.3	8.7	9.8	8.2	13.0	8.8	10.5	9.9 (9)	10.9 (9)
Leather, fur, clothing and footwear	5.4	4.1	10.6	5.2	6.7	5.6	10.6	9.8	11.3	10.6	8.9 (10)	7.1 (11)
Paper, printing and publishing	5.2	4.4	5.1	6.0	5.2	6.5	5.5	9.7	6.0	11.3	5.4 (11)	7.6 (10)
Food, drink and tobacco	4.5	1.6	4.0	2.2	4.2	2.1	4.7	4.0	5.7	5.8	4.6 (12)	3.2 (13)
Timber and furniture	1.4	4.2	1.3	5.0	1.6	5.8	1.6	9.7	2.1	8.2	1.6 (13)	6.6 (12)
Total manufacturing	13.6	14.3	14.1	17.2	13.7	17.9	14.5	23.9	15.2	24.3	14.2	19.5

SOURCE: Panic.

TABLE 7

The importance of large plants in the manufacturing industries of West Germany and the UK, 1958 and 1968

	No. of large plants		Ratio of UK to WG average size of large plants	Percentage of total employment in large plants		No. of large plants		Ratio of UK to WG average size of large plants	Percentage of total employment in large plants	
	UK	WG		UK	WG	UK	WG		UK	WG
Food, drink and tobacco	110	32	113	29.9	11.0	134	46	118	32.0	13.8
Chemicals and allied industries	82	82	66	40.8	59.7	90	103	60	41.4	61.2
Engineering and electrical goods	336	325	96	44.2	47.7	384	425	83	39.8	46.2
Shipbuilding and marine engineering	64	17	61	67.2	72.5	35	15	85	63.3	76.8
Vehicles and aircraft	184	60	73	75.1	78.5	168	86	65	73.7	82.8
Metal goods nes	35	47	94	11.9	15.6	53	43	82	16.0	12.9
Metal manufacturing	114	153	67	51.8	59.8	105	154	90	53.2	58.4
Textiles	49	73	113	10.6	19.0	61	57	106	15.6	17.3
Leather, fur, clothing and footwear	18	28	80	4.9	11.1	21	17	115	6.4	4.3
Bricks, pottery, glass and cement	30	35	106	17.8	13.1	35	35	90	20.6	15.4
Timber and furniture	3	9	127	2.2	4.3	3	8	80	1.4	4.1
Paper, printing and publishing	65	20	120	21.1	8.4	69	33	106	20.5	12.2
Other manufacturing	38	35	91	30.8	34.1	40	43	92	27.5	30.9
All manufacturing	1128	916	92	34.1	34.4	1198	1065	85	34.5	36.5

SOURCE: Panic.

TABLE 8

Annual % Rates of Growth in Output (Value Added) per Person Employed (Output Measured at 1963 Factor Costs)

Average Annual Percentage Compound Growth Rates

	From 1950–52 to 1958–60	From 1958–60 to 1967–69
Belgium	4.0	5.6
Germany ...	5.9	5.6
France......	4.5	6.0
Italy........	6.0	6.2
Holland	4.5	6.1
Switzerland .	2.1	3.4
UK	2.3	3.2

SOURCE: Economic Survey of Europe in 1971; United Nations.

TABLE 9

Output/capital ratios in manufacturing in major developed countries, 1957-76

Ratio of gross value added to gross capital stock (per cent)

	1957	1962	1967	1972	1973	1974	1975	1976
UK	38.8	38.2	36.4	33.3	32.3	29.6	28.3	26.5
USA	78.0	83.3	89.0	78.0	80.7	76.1	71.9	76.8
Japan	53.2	58.9	59.5	55.1	52.8	45.6	45.2	–
Germany	56.3	53.6	48.6	48.7	50.0	49.3	46.0	47.9
Italy	28.5	30.0	30.2	30.8	–	–	–	–
Sweden	40.1	39.2	36.9	35.4	35.7	38.2	37.2	35.9

SOURCE: T. P. Hill, *Profits and Rates of Return* (OECD, 1979).

TABLE 10

Incremental output/capital ratios in manufacturing in major developed countries

Increase in value added divided by investment at constant prices in manufacturing industry over the period.

	Period[1]	Index: UK = 100
UK	1958–72	100
USA	1958–71	147
Japan	1962–72	157
France......	1960–71	163
Germany ...	1958–72	190
Sweden	1960–73	145

1. The period of comparison for each country has been chosen to eliminate distortions due to cyclical influences.

SOURCE: CBI evidence; also Treasury Economic Progress Report Supplement, March, 1979.

TABLE 11

Growth of labour productivity in UK and West German manufacturing industries, 1954-72, per cent per annum

Industry	1954–59		1959–63		1963–68		1968–72		1954–72	
	UK	WG	UK	WG	UK	WG	UK	WG	UK	WG
Food	0.9	2.5	1.5	2.9	2.7	4.5	2.9	3.4	2.0	3.4
Drink and tobacco	2.9	7.2	2.6	6.7	4.8	6.3	3.6	4.7	3.5	6.3
Chemicals and allied industries	4.5	6.4	5.2	7.8	6.9	10.0	5.1	5.5	5.4	7.5
Metal manufacturing	1.2	2.0	0.9	1.8	2.6	6.4	1.0	3.0	1.5	3.4
Engineering and electrical goods	1.4	2.0	1.8	2.6	4.4	4.2	3.4	4.3	2.8	3.2
Shipbuilding and marine engineering	1.6	-0.2	1.7	1.1	-0.2	7.3	-1.3	3.1	0.5	2.9
Vehicles and aircraft	4.1	6.9	1.4	6.4	4.7	1.2	0.7	3.1	2.9	4.3
Metal goods n.e.s.	0.5	2.3	-0.1	4.0	1.9	4.1	0.1	5.9	0.7	4.0
Textiles	1.7	4.5	3.0	5.9	6.1	6.5	5.7	6.5	4.7	5.8
Leather, fur, clothing and footwear	1.6	3.4	0.2	2.4	2.4	4.4	3.2	2.9	1.9	3.3
Bricks, pottery, glass and cement	1.7	4.6	3.8	6.3	4.9	5.7	5.4	4.5	3.9	5.3
Timber and furniture	3.8	4.1	2.3	4.9	2.3	6.9	3.7	7.2	3.0	5.7
Paper, printing and publishing	1.4	2.1	0.2	3.3	3.0	5.5	2.5	4.3	1.8	3.8
Other manufacturing	2.5	3.2	4.0	5.1	4.6	6.5	2.1	5.3	3.3	5.0
Total manufacturing	2.2	3.6	2.0	4.3	4.2	5.8	3.1	4.5	2.9	4.6
Coefficient of variation	0.562	0.562	0.740	0.457	0.495	0.342	0.726	0.293	0.492	0.293

SOURCES: UK – Central Statistical Office; Department of Employment; and Cambridge University Department of Applied Economics *op. cit.* West Germany – Deutsches Institut für Wirtschaftsforschung.

TABLE 12

Relationships between concentration and net output per worker, UK, 1970

5-firm Concentration Ratio	Product Group (Minimum List Heading) Average Net Output per Worker	Number of Product Groups (Minimum List Headings)
%	£	
0–10	1938.8	5
11–20	1919.1	12
21–30	2111.0	23
31–40	2222.4	25
41–50	2587.8	25
51–60	2748.1	16
61–70	2792.6	9
71–80	3582.4	8
81–90	3053.9	10
91–100	2474.3	4
		137

SOURCE: Census Data, 1970

TABLE 13

Comparison of the average net output per worker in each product group (MLH) and for the largest 5 firms in each product group, UK, 1970

5-firm Concentration Ratio	Product Group (MLH) Average Net Output per Worker	5 largest firms in product group average net output per Worker
%	£	£
0–10	1938.8	2202.0
11–20	1919.1	1990.5
21–30	2111.0	2159.7
31–40	2222.4	2316.0
41–50	2587.8	2871.6
51–60	2748.1	2699.4
61–70	2792.6	3623.9
71–80	3582.4	3631.1
81–90	3053.9	2953.6
91–100	2474.3	2434.0

SOURCE: Census Data, 1970

TABLE 14

Saving and investment in major developed countries, 1973-77

Per cent of GDP at market prices

	Saving[1]	Investment[2]
UK	17.0	20.0
USA	17.3	17.8
Japan	32.6	33.6
France	21.1	24.5
Germany	23.6	22.3
Italy	21.8	23.0

1. Gross saving, before deducting capital consumption.
2. Increase in stocks *plus* gross fixed capital formation.

SOURCE: National Accounts of OECD Countries, 1960-1977

TABLE 15

Investment in the UK by the enterprise sector, 1958-79

Per cent of GDP at market prices

	1958-62	1963-67	1968-72	1973-77	1978	1979
Gross domestic fixed capital formation:						
Industrial and comcercial companies	6.5	6.5	6.2	6.8	6.9	6.4
Financial companies and institutions	0.4	0.7	1.2	1.7	2.0	2.1
Public corporations	3.2	3.7	3.2	3.5	3.1	2.9
Personal sector (excluding dwellings)	1.3	1.0	1.3	1.0	1.5	1.7
Total enterprise sector	11.4	11.9	12.0	12.9	13.4	13.1
of which: manufacturing	*4.1*	*3.8*	*3.8*	*3.4*	*3.6*	*3.5*
Value of physical increase in stocks and work in progress:						
Total enterprise sector	0.9	1.1	0.6	0.6	0.6	1.7
Gross domestic capital formation by the enterprise sector	12.3	13.0	12.6	13.6	14.0	14.8

SOURCE: National Income and Expenditure, 1979 Edition; Economic Trends

TABLE 16

International comparison of profitability, 1960-78

Net pre-tax rates of return[1]; annual averages; per cent

	1960-62	1963-67	1968-71	1972-75	1976-78
Manufacturing industry					
UK.............	15	14	11	6	4
USA	27	36	26	22	24
Canada........	19	18	16	17	13
Germany........	29	21	22	16	–
Non-financial corporations					
UK.............	11	10	8	4	4
USA	18	22	18	15	15
France..........	11	12	15	13	–

1. Net operating surplus (gross trading surplus before tax net of replacement cost depreciation and stock appreciation) as per cent of net stock of fixed capital at current replacement cost.

SOURCE: T. P. Hill, *Profits and Rates of Return* (OECD, 1979); updated by the author

TABLE 17

Probability of surviving for a ten-year period for companies existing in 1960

Size group	Boundary (£m)	Probability of survival	Probability of being taken over	Probability of liquidation
1	65>	0.73	0.27	0.00
2	35-65	0.80	0.20	0.00*
3	15-35	0.73	0.27	0.00
4	10-15	0.67	0.33	0.00
5	5-10	0.73	0.27	0.00
6	2.5-5	0.50	0.50	0.00
7	1-2.5	0.59	0.41	0.00
8	0.5-1 0.57	0.57 0.38	·0.38 0.05	0.05
9	0.25-0.5	0.42	0.48	0.10
10	<0.25	0.42	0.41	0.17

* Including Rolls-Royce

TABLE 18

Mortality ratios among small firms

	Manufacturing of construction	Wholesale	Motor	Retail
Liquidation	8%	19%	8%	15%
Ceasing to trade	2%	6%	5%	9%
Taken over	13%	8%	5%	4%
Total deaths	23%	33%	19%	28%

Percentage of small firms in existence in 1963 going into liquidation, ceasing to trade or taken over by 1970 – that is, estimates of probabilities for an eight-year period.

References

1. *Bolton Committee of Inquiry on Small Firms*, Cmnd 4811, HMSO, 1972: *Committee to review the functioning of financial institutions* (Wilson Committee) Cmnd 7937, HMSO, 1980.
2. Hannah, L., and Kay, J. A., 'The contribution of mergers to concentration of growth: a reply to Professor Hart' in the *Journal of Industrial Economics*, March, 1981.
3. Hart, P. E., 'The effects of mergers on industrial concentration'. *Ibid.*
4. Prais, S. J., 'The contribution of mergers to industrial concentration: what do we know?' *Ibid.*
5. Whittington, G., 'The profitability and size of UK companies, 1960 –1974', *The Journal of Industrial Economics*, June, 1980, pp. 335 –352.
6. Singh, A., *Takeovers, their relevance to the stock market and the theory of the firm*, Cambridge University Press, London, 1971.
7. Newbould, G. D., *Management and merger activity*, Guthstead, Liverpool, 1970.
8. Meeks, G., *Disappointing marriage: a study of the gains from merger*, Cambridge University Press, London, 1977.

CHAPTER 3

Economics and small enterprises

Brian Hindley

I Introduction

Economists interested in industrial structure spend much of their time thinking about size of enterprise, but usually about bigness and the problems associated with it rather than about smallness as such. Hostility to bigness of firms relative to markets has a long and honourable history in economics, and the analysis on which that hostility is founded – the resource allocation consequences of monopoly – is very clear. It doesn't follow, of course, that a passion for resource allocation has invariably been the primary motivation of anti-monopoly economists; and one might suspect that monopoly has sometimes served as a stalking horse for a variety of other social concerns with a less precise rationale, including an aversion to great size as such, whether relative to markets or not. Nevertheless, absolute size has become an explicit focus for concern and research among economists only relatively recently.

Both of these traditions are powerful and intriguing to economists, and it is perhaps useful to make the simple point that anti-bigness does not logically imply a position in favour of genuine smallness and that to be pro-small, it is not necessary to be anti-big. The two states can co-exist. In fact they *do* co-exist, as Table 4 makes clear. Moreover, the data given there refers only to manufacturing. In recent years, there has been a shift of employment from manufacturing to services, where small units are more common. One might expect this shift to continue in the future.

Indeed, to emphasise the point, it may be that an active anti-big policy militates also against the existence of genuinely small firms. On the basis of the available evidence, it is quite plausible that many very large firms could be broken into smaller units without economic loss and even with economic gain. But the smaller units would still be large – not intimate size; and if prices were lower and competition harder, if there was more expenditure on research and development, and if innovations were adopted more rapidly, this may be good for resource allocation, but it is not clear that such conditions favour the existence of really small firms.

This possibility is introduced here simply to stress the distinction between positions that could be confused. However, before pursuing quasi-philosophical issues any further, it is worth surveying several pieces of evidence on comparative industrial structure. There have been recently a variety of useful studies which give a much sharper feel for divergent possibilities than any amount of dataless discussion.

II Comparative industrial structure

In the present context, the first point to stress is the distinction between enterprises and establishments. We tend to think in terms of vast enterprises, and for many purposes that is quite appropriate. From the point of view of workers and the work-place, however, it can be quite misleading.

Thus, in 1963 the 200 largest manufacturing enterprises in the US produced 41% of that nation's manufacturing output; but they produced it in some 9000 plants (an average of 45 each), and each of these plants employed, on average, 580 persons. In the UK a similar share of manufacturing output was accounted for by 125 firms. On average, these controlled 33 plants each, and the average employment in such plants was 640 persons.[1]

To put the same point in a different way, half of the UK manufacturing labour force in 1968 was employed in *enterprises* with more than 3000 employees. But also, half of the UK manufacturing labour force was employed in *plants* with total employment less than 480. In the US in 1967, the figures were 1500 for enterprises and 420 for plants. Moreover, these figures conceal substantial inter-industry variation. Table 1 gives a more disaggregated view[2].

Comparisons with respect to employment in plant (though not in enterprises) can be extended across several countries and years. Table 2 gives three measures: the average number of employees per establishment, the percentage of employees in establishments with more than 500 persons, and the percentage of employees in establishments with more than 200 persons.[3]

Among the four major European powers every indication is that plant is smaller in France than in the UK or Germany (whose overall plant structure is remarkably similar to that of the UK) and that Italian plant is smaller than French. Thus, George and Ward[4] arrange a sample of 47 comparable industries in descending order of the average employment size of the twenty largest plants in the UK industry. The results are reproduced here as Table 3.

Intra-European comparison of enterprise establishment structure is not straightforward: the presentation of official statistics does not allow them to be. However, there are strong indications that despite the similarity of *plant* structure between Germany and the UK, British firms on average operate more plants and are substantially larger. In studies of the largest manufacturing enterprises in the EEC the UK tends to have up to twice as many representatives as Germany (moreover, in terms of *sales*, given the substantially higher German productivity, the discrepancy must be even greater in terms of employment), Germany more than France, and France more than Italy. At a less aggregated level, George and Ward divide the average employment size of the four largest firms in 41 comparable industries by the average size of the four largest plants. Their unweighted averages are 2.5 for the UK, 1.56 for Germany, and 1.75 for France. Scherer's detailed study of 12 industries gives further support. The average number of plants operated by the three largest firms in his sample industries was: US 11.9; Canada 4.2; UK 6.4; Sweden 2.6; France 6.8; and Germany 5.1.[5]

Similar comparisons are not possible for Japan. However, the Industrial Policy Group reported on the distribution by employment of the size of manufacturing companies in Japan: in 1966, 16.0% of the manufacturing labour force was employed in enterprises having more than 1000 employees as against 14.6% in 1955; 14.2% were employed in enterprises employing between 300 and 1000 as against 12.4% 11 years earlier; and 69.8% were employed in enterprises having less than 300 employees, down from 73% at the earlier date. The shift towards larger enterprises suggested by these figures is confirmed from another source: in 1962, Japan had 31 representatives in Fortune's list of the 200 largest non-American manufacturing companies and in 1972, 51 representatives.[6]

Both Tables 1 and 3 suggest a considerable correspondence between *relative* size of plant in different industries compared across countries. This correspondence is confirmed, at both plant and firm level by a variety of studies, both examining this issue directly and also indirectly by correlating concentration ratios across countries. We have studies linking the US and the UK;[7] the US and Japan;[8] the UK and the EEC;[9] and different members of the six[10]; while Pryor[11] analyses both relative plant size and concentration across a broader range of economies.

These findings are important insofar as they suggest a strong technological influence on industry structure. Scherer's recent work has furthered this view by statistically explaining a good deal of the observed and ostensibly different national divergences between minimum optimal scale of plant (MOS) and actual size in terms of such variables as size of market, transport costs, and the curvature of the unit cost curve at non-optimal scales. Statistically, his 6 nation, 12 industry sample could have been drawn from the same population, which implies that nationality is not an important variable in determining plant size: a conclusion, however, that Scherer himself is inclined to disavow.

However, this is far from the end of the story: sharp differences tend to emerge as one moves from the big end of the size scale to the small end. This is most clearly seen in Prais' comparison of manufacturing establishments employing under 10 persons, reproduced here as Table 4. Some rough idea of the Japanese position emerges from Elliott and Hughes, who compare a figure for 1967 of 3% for the proportion of US manufacturing employment in such establishments with 16% for Japan (and who also note that the Japanese figure had been 23% in 1954).[12]

Looking at particular comparable categories is in some senses even more impressive. For example, Germany had 22,674 such enterprises engaged in furniture production, Britain 924; Germany 39,080 in metal products, Britain 4,480; Germany 5,730 in precision and optical instruments, Britain 736.

There are several curiosities in this data, but I want to focus on one – the position of the UK. Why, after all, should the UK have fewer small establishments – whether less than 10 employees or less than 200 – than the other countries listed?

Evidently, the answer could lie in differences in the institutional structure of economies: different capital market structures or levels or forms of taxation. However, I want to examine pure economic possibilities. Thus, for example, technological factors could in principle explain the difference, though this seems unlikely. As we have seen, there is strong evidence of common technological factors playing a major role in the determination of industrial structure at the large end of the scale. Why at the other end should they operate so differently and how to explain the difference in numbers of small enterprises in the UK, Belgium and the Netherlands, France and Germany? Overall German plant structure is very similar to that of the UK at the larger end of the scale, but appears to diverge significantly at the smaller end: can differences in technology explain why the German manufacturing sector can support triple the number of very small firms as that of the UK? It seems implausible. One is more inclined to link the differences in small enterprises at one end of the scale to the differences in establishment-enterprise structure at the other and to suggest that the British economy has a smaller supply of persons willing or able to become final decision takers.

An alternative answer could lie in differences in the composition of output – different trades call for different scales of plant, so that differences in industrial structure as a whole could result from differences in output of small plant and large plant industries. This again seems unlikely between the UK and Germany, where the composition of output appears remarkably similar.[13] Moreover, once the possibility of different preferences is introduced, the composition of output contention begs a more fundamental question: whether small firms exist because the composition of output is what it is, or whether the composition of output is what it is because there are small firms. One can either move from standard comparative cost considerations to the result that particular countries are favoured for industries congenial to small firms; or one could argue from a preference for small firms to the existence of industries congenial to them.

In any event, there are two reasons for pursuing the idea of different preferences. The first is intrinsic interest. The second is that this is an exercise with a strong normative component – there is a presumption in favour of small enterprises.

III Preferences and industrial structure

I propose a very simple model. Suppose that we have a single product economy but two available fixed proportion techniques of production: the big plant technique and the small plant technique. We can suppose that in all relevant circumstances, big plants are used and dominate production, and it simplifies matters if we assume that the price of output and the wage paid in large plants are given.

In the simplest version, there are now three factors determining the plant size distribution. First, workers' preferences with respect to size reflect themselves in a supply function of labour to the small plant sector:

(1) $W_s = W(N_s)$ $W' \geq 0$

where N_s is the number of small plants. Second, the preferences of potential entrepreneurs yield the supply of entrepreneurs to the small plant sector as a function of the rate of profit in that sector.

(2) $N_s = N(\pi_s)$ $N' \geq 0$

Finally, the fixed coefficient production function, given prices, permits profits to be expressed as a function of wage rates:

$$\pi_s = (W_s) \qquad \pi' < 0$$

The three equations and three variables solve to a determinate number of small plants (and, of course, of W_s and π_s). One such solution is illustrated in Figure 1.

The first point to make is about the notion of economic efficiency. Once the idea of preferences with respect to size of working unit is introduced, very little can be deduced about efficiency from economic variables alone. Thus, one might observe that output per man in the small plant sector is one half output per man in the large plant sector: that is consistent with economic efficiency. One might observe that wages are less in the small plant sector, and that also is compatible with economic efficiency. Moreover, nothing could be

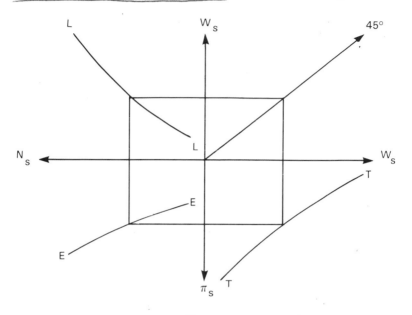

Figure 1

inferred about comparative efficiency if one country possessed a tiny small firm sector and another, with similar technology, a much larger one.

Second, the size of the small plant sector is determined *jointly* by technology and preferences. Thus, if technology shifts in favour of large plants – which would cause an inward shift of TT in quadrant II of Figure 1 – while preferences are unchanged, the outcome will be a reduction in the number of small plants and a reduction of entrepreneurial earnings and wages in that sector. However, if workers' preferences shift in favour of small plants (LL in quadrant IV shifts downward), there will be more small plants, an increase in small plant entrepreneurial wealth, and a reduction in small plant wages: to attract more entrepreneurs with given technology, profits must rise and wages fall. But if the supply of potential entrepreneurs increases (EE in quadrant III shifts downward), there will be an increase in small plant wages and a reduction in entrepreneurial earnings. In principle, whatever the technological gap between small and large plants, preferences sufficiently strongly biased towards small plants could result in an economy dominated by small plants.

It would be reasonable to query whether any of this analysis has other than an 'in principle' significance – after all, industrial economists trying to explain plant structure have not resorted to such a preference approach. To such a query, there are two responses.

First, one might be quite content with in principle propositions. The point is that *if* preferences with respect to size were very strong relative to the technological superiority of scale, we should expect the preferences to be significant in industrial structure. If preferences are not a significant determinant, one possible implication is that they are not very strong. But in any case, statistical analysis of the determinants of sizes of plant across countries leaves quite a lot of variance unexplained – empirically, what industrial economists think is important does not preclude the relevance of other factors. Why does one observe large and apparently systematic differences in establishment size between countries at similar levels of technological development? The question continues to concern Scherer, despite his good statistical results.

Second, though there is no empirical evidence of any effect of preferences on industrial structure, there is evidence of the existence of worker preferences with respect to scale. It has been known for a long time that wage rates in small firms were on average lower than those in larger firms; but such crude comparisons confound the effects of varieties of other factors affecting wages: for example, different skill mixes between large and small firms, different rates of unionisation, different rates of female employment.

However, the size effect remains statistically significant in a variety of reported multiple regression analyses controlling for such variation. Most importantly, in a study published in 1976 of the supply of labour, Metcalfe et al,[14] using simultaneous equations, report that the size variable remained significant in the *supply* equation even when bargaining proxies were independently included; and this strongly suggests that at least part of the reported scale effect on wages derives from preferences with respect to size.

George et al.[15] have published a survey (in 1977) of results and theory pertaining to size of establishment and labour market behaviour. On the basis of the surveyed empirical results, they conclude that an increase in plant size of 250 workers would lead to an increase in average hourly earnings of about 2.5%, and a decrease in hours supplied of about one hour per week.

Whether these figures are large or small depends upon their value relative to technology. Scherer *et al.* give estimates of minimum optimal scale for 12 industries, and also the cost disadvantage of a plant constructed at one-third of that scale. The plausibility of the estimates is enhanced by their statistical significance on his own regressions explaining observed plant size as a fraction of MOS. The estimates range from 1.5% in non-rubber shoes and 2.2% in cigarettes to 26.0% in Portland cement. Clearly in non-rubber shoes and cigarettes, worker preferences with respect to scale of the magnitude reported could play a significant role: in Portland cement, they are unlikely to.

However, the situation is somewhat more complicated than this. George *et al.* also report that the quit rate appears to fall by 1% for an increase in firm size of 10%; and that for an industry employing more than 100,000, an increase in average firm size of 100 workers will reduce strike frequency by one strike per annum. They also note that there is some evidence from the US that expenditure on labour relations per employee rises with size. Clearly these observations are likely to be connected, and raise the question of what is the cost of avoiding the extra strike or quit. Nevertheless, the evidence here is ambiguous with respect to the benefits of small scale.

IV Conclusion

It is easy to obtain a distorted picture of the scale and impersonality of the typical work-place. Huge production line establishments, such as occur in the automobile assembly industry, are the exception not the rule. Even in a steel mill, vast though it may be, men work in small teams dealing directly with a quite limited and personal management structure. Moreover, the figures cited earlier exaggerate scale, since they refer to manufacturing alone. By 1960, none of the advanced economies of the West employed as much as 50% of their labour force in manufacturing. In 1974, only 30% of the US labour force was so employed; 30% of the Canadian; 40% of the Belgian; 38% of the French; 44% of the Italian; 36% of the Swedish and Japanese; 47% of the German; and 41% of the British. The range of choice with respect to size of work-place is very broad.

That is not to say, of course, that the range of choice is wide enough. Taxes and capital markets may well discriminate against small organisations; and the problems of large organisations are more evident and politically charged, and official bureaucrats might have more fellow feeling for their opposite numbers in large private organisations, and the opposite numbers more skill and practice in exploiting a bureaucracy than the probably less polished managers of small enterprises.

This may well be the case in Britain, for example. To construct a case that the technological space for small enterprise in Britain is greater than that used is much easier, in terms of comparative analysis, than to build a case that Britain's economic problems stem from an unduly small scale of production. Yet insofar as Whitehall acts in the matter of scale, it acts on the latter proposition. That is not to say that Whitehall is solely responsible for the relative lack of small enterprise: on the contrary, it may well be that it is in large part a sociological phenomenon, reflecting itself through what economists call preferences and bound up with other peculiarities of the British economy. Nevertheless, official *de facto* discrimination could not help the situation; and it would be an absurdity if bureaucratic neatness of mind were allowed to triumph over entrepreneurial disorder.

TABLE 1

Plant-sizes by industry, United Kingdom (1968) and United States (1967)

	Florence-median[1]		Small plants[2]		Large plants[3]	
	UK	US	UK	US	UK	US
	No. of employees		(Percentages)			
Food, drink and tobacco	510	210	*9*	*19*	*12*	*4*
Chemicals and allied industries	740	540	*8*	*12*	*19*	*20*
Metal manufacture	1180	1480	*6*	*5*	*34*	*40*
Engineering and electrical goods	710	750	*10*	*11*	*16*	*24*
Shipbuilding and marine engineering	2600	1380	*6*	*8*	*51*	*46*
Vehicles	3000	6000	*3*	*2*	*55*	*68*
Metal goods n.e.s.	220	230	*23*	*19*	*2*	*8*
Textiles	280	450	*10*	*9*	*4*	*9*
Leather, leather goods and fur	120	140	*35*	*26*	–	*3*
Clothing and footwear	180	200	*21*	*17*	*1*	*1*
Bricks, pottery, glass, cement, etc.	300	180	*18*	*26*	*4*	*3*
Timber and furniture	90	120	*37*	*30*	–	*1*
Paper, printing, publishing	290	240	*19*	*20*	*7*	*6*
Other manufacturing	370	280	*15*	*16*	*14*	*6*
Total manufacturing	480	420	*12*	*14*	*17*	*20*

SOURCES: United Kingdom: *Censuses of Production;* United States: *Censuses of Manufactures.*

(United States industries reclassified for comparability with the United Kingdoms.)

[1] Half of all employees in plants below that size, and half above.
[2] Under 50 employees (and including all unsatisfactory returns for the United Kingdom).
[3] 2500 employees and over.

TABLE 2

Average number of employees per establishment, and percentage of employees in manufacturing employed in establishments with more than 500 employees and with less than 200 employees[16]

	Average employees per establishment	Per cent in est. with more than 500 employees	Per cent in est. with less than 200 employees	
	(1963–64)	(1963–64)	1953[a]	1963[a]
UK[b]	144	51	33	31
Germany	136	50	40	34
USA[b]	82	43	37	39
Canada	66	33	46	47
Belgium	–	–	–	51
France	–	–	58	51
Sweden	74	31	56	53
Japan	52	33	59	54
Netherlands	–	–	–	58
Australia	37	25	62	60
Switzerland	–	–	66	61
Norway	–	–	70	65
Italy	–	–	–	66

a   Or closest available date
b   In the UK, the number of small establishments has halved since the 1930s. In the US, the number has roughly doubled.[16]

TABLE 3

Average size of the 20 largest plants by industry groups, UK, Germany, France and Italy

Average size of plant ('000)

Industry group[a]	UK	Germany	France	Italy
A(10)	4.65	5.51	3.04	1.64
B(10)	1.92	1.80	0.79	0.77
C(9)	1.26	1.34	0.68	0.66
D(9)	0.73	0.72	0.43	0.41
E(9)	0.38	0.50	0.32	0.20

a   The 47 industries are arranged in descending order of their size in the UK and divided into groups of 9 or 10.

TABLE 4

Manufacturing establishments^a employing under ten persons, United Kingdom compared with other countries, 1963

	Small establishments^b		Proportion of total manufacturing employment
	Number	Per 1000 manufacturing employees	
	(000s)		(%)
UK	27	4	*2.1*
US	121	6	*2.4*
France	186	31	*10.8*
Germany	157	15	*6.2*
Italy	245	42	18.5
Benelux	57	23	*8.7*

SOURCES: United Kingdom: *Census of Production, 1963*; United States: *Census of Manufactures, 1963*; EEC – *Industriezensus, 1963.*

a   Excludes certain branches of manufacturing bordering on service trades.

b   Defined for the United Kingdom as one with 1–10 employees, for elsewhere as one with 1–9 employees. British figures therefore slightly overstated in comparison.

References

1. Prais, S. J., *The evolution of giant firms in Britain* (Cambridge University Press, 1976).
2. *Ibid.*
3. Industrial Policy Group, *The structure and efficiency of British industry* (London, 1970).
4. George, Kenneth and Ward, T. S., *The structure of industry in the EEC* (Cambridge University Press, 1976).
5. Scherer, F. M. *et al*, *The economics of multi-plant operation* (Harvard, 1975).
6. Jaquemin, Alex and Saez, W., 'A comparison of the performance of the largest European and Japanese industrial firms', *Oxford Economic Papers*, July, 1976.
7. Pashigian, P., 'Market concentration in the United States and Great Britain', *Journal of Law and Economics*, 1968.
8. Caves, Richard and Uekusa, Masu, 'Industrial organisation' in Hugh Patrick and Henry Rosovsky (eds.), *Asia's new giant* (Brookings, 1976).
9. George and Ward, *op cit.*
10. Phillips, L., *Effects of industrial concentration: a cross-section analysis for the common market* (North Holland, 1971).
11. Pryor, F. L., 'An international comparison of concentration ratios', *Review of Economics and Statistics*, May, 1972 and 'Size of production establishments in manufacturing', *Economic Journal*, June, 1972.
12. Elliott, Ian and Hughes, Alan, 'Capital and labour: their growth, distribution and productivity' in M. Panic (Ed.) *The UK and West German manufacturing industry 1954–72* (London, NEDO, 1976).
13. *Ibid.*
14. Metcalf, D., Nickell, S., and Richardson, R., 'The structure of hours and earnings in British Manufacturing Industry', *Oxford Economic Papers*, 1976.
15. George, Kenneth *et al*, 'The size of the work unit and labour market behaviour', *British Journal of Industrial Relations*, No. 2, 1977.
16. *Bolton Committee of Inquiry on small firms* (HMSO, London, 1972, cmnd. 4811).

See also: Horowitz, I., 'Employment concentration in the Common Market: an entropy approach', *Journal of the Royal Statistical Society*, Series A, 1970.

CHAPTER 4

A new model of the process of business concentration

Robin Marris

This chapter presents a model of the process of business concentration – by which is meant the process whereby large units *in general* acquire increasing control of the total assets and output of the private sector – based on a theory of internal growth and a theory of mergers. We are interested in business concentration because, *inter alia*, the growth of large units reduces the scope for small and medium-sized units. (Some realism is required; given that large units are generally more capital intensive than small units, and given the extreme skewness of the size-distribution, a system that is highly concentrated in terms of output or assets may still display a substantial proportion of employment in small units; it is therefore important to know whether our interest in small units is primarily economic, political or sociological.)

Despite some controversy surrounding the matter, the variance of the natural logs of the sizes of firms is taken as a measure of concentration. It is possible to create examples where this logarithmic variance will move in the opposite direction to more familiar measures of concentration, such as the share of output or assets taken by the top 100, top 200, etc. But most such examples are really examples of processes of industrial concentration, eg of a train of events in a single industry where, as a result of intra-industry mergers, increased shares for one group of firms is associated with reduced output shares for other groups within the same industry. In the models simulated as background to this chapter, which were based on large, multi-industry populations of at least 1000 firms, the conventional concentration ratios vary linearly with the *log* of the logarithmic variance itself. (Let X_{it} be the natural log of the size of firm i at time t and let o^2_{xt} represent the variance of these numbers. Then if C_2 is the share of the aggregate size of the whole population accounted for by the top 2% of units, C_2 tended to increase linearly at a constant rate over time. Log o^2_{xt}, after a period of acceleration, then converged to a constant linear rate of increase approximately equal to that of C_2.)

The use of logarithmic variance as a measure of concentration has significant policy implications, some of which will be discussed further, later. If one's interest in small units is primarily sociological, one will wish to encourage units whose absolute size is small, especially small units that are labour intensive. The same may or may not hold if one's interest is directly political. But if one's interest is strictly economic, for example if one believes that excessive concentration either reduces the general degree of competition in the economy (which is, incidentally, by no means obvious) or if, from a mixture of economic and political motives, one fears an excessive concentration of economic power, one may find that the best policy is to encourage units the log of whose sizes is only moderately below the mean logarithmic size; in a skew distribution which becomes more symmetrical under a log transform, such units will be, although smaller than the mean absolute size, considerably larger than the smallest absolute-sized units. The types of practical policies, institutional arrangements etc appropriate to this type of policy are notably different from those required for the sociological type of policy.

The merger model

Despite a considerable literature, no previous theory has specified the merger process as one with stable transition matrices defined in terms of the probabilities of firms of size X acquiring firms of size Y. (J. McGowan, Yale Economic Papers, 1966, employed a one-time, empirically determined transition matrix for the probability of a firm of size X migrating to size Y, which contains the basis of the idea we have employed here and is related to it in the sense of containing an implicit matrix of the kind we have defined, but did not follow our general approach.) In the present case, firms are arranged in logarithmic size classes and mergers are divided into 'major' and 'minor'. A major merger is one that immediately takes the acquiring firm out of its size class, in the sense that the sum of the acquired and acquiring firms lies above the limits of the size-class of the acquiring firm on the date immediately preceding the merger. All other mergers are minor mergers. The effect of minor mergers on the sizes of acquiring firms is treated as part of the theory of internal growth. The present section is concerned with major mergers.

We define a matrix P_j to represent the probabilities that firms in logarithmic size classes defined in the columns will, during a given period, acquire one firm of size class indicated in the rows. From this we may derive the matrix P, such that if N_t is a column vector signifying the (logarithmic) size distribution at time t, immediately before any major mergers have taken place, while N_{t+1} is the corresponding distribution immediately after all the major mergers of the period have taken place, $N_{t+1} = PN_t$. Clearly, the P-matrix is similar to McGowan's matrix.

The 15-period (15-year) simulation on which our account is based employed a P_j matrix constructed on the assumption that the relevant probabilities were approximately normally distributed across the rows: firms were most likely to acquire other firms about 60% of their own absolute size (with a probability of 4%) with correspondingly declining figures on either side of this mode, so that, for example, the probability of a firm's acquiring one firm in its own size class was one half or 1%. The precise figures are given in Appendix 1.

The effects of this matrix were simulated over 15 transitions from an initial size distribution of 1,000 firms which, though approximately log-normal, was only very slightly concentrated. The initial value of o^2_x was only a little over .05 and the initial value of C_2 (the top 2% concentration ratio) was about 1%. After a few years, as indicated, the process settled down to a state of affairs where the *log* of the logarithmic variance (ie log o^2_x) was growing at a constant rate of 0.07 and the C_2 concentration ratio was growing at a constant rate of one percentage point per annum. The final value of the concentration ratio (which would, of course, be the 200-firm ratio in a population of 10,000) after fifteen years was a few points short of 20%. In the United States at the present time the 200-firm ratio in terms of value added is about 50%, in terms of assets about 63%.

The probabilities employed in the assumed P_j matrix imply a rather faster overall rate of merger than is found on average in data relating to large US corporations from 1900 to the present day, but is not very much larger than values observed in periods of intense merger activity, or so-called 'merger-waves'. Inasmuch as we are concerned with a process that operates through long periods of time, it would be advisable to regard the simulation figures as representing a process that is too strong for empirical reality by a factor of two. In other words, instead of taking fifteen years to reach a C_2 ratio of 20%, we might imagine that typical US conditions of the present century would imply a rate of growth of concentration, due to major-merger only, such that instead of adding 20 points every fifteen years, as in the simulation, the same result takes 30 or 40 years.

The annual increase in o^2_x (not log o^2_x) is to be signified by m. In the simulation, because o^2_x is following a log-linear law, m is not constant through times, but for illustration it may be observed that half its average value over the whole 15-year simulation period works out at rather less than .05. In what follows, m (rightly or wrongly) is treated as a constant.

The effects of internal growth

We make use of a theory of the internal growth of the firm that is a development of models we have published elsewhere, more especially in the *Economic Journal*, May, 1972. This is a steady-state model for the long-run growth of the firm based on the assumption that by annually spending an amount, normalised by assets, eg, a firm can grow exponentially at the rate g while sustaining, on each successive project, an internal operating profit rate $\hat{p}$ that is constant through time, taking one project with another. All growth is internally financed. The management aims either to maximise the normalised stock market value of the firm, v, or to maximise the growth rate g, subject to the value of v not falling below the value of the firm to some raider who values it on the assumption that its future growth rate, rather than g, will be zero; or the firm adopts some mixture of these two motivational extremes. The mixture adopted is defined by a motivational index M, lying at or between the extreme values of $1/2$ for the Max-v case and 1.0 for the Max-g case. In turn the stock exchange values the firm on the assumption that the expected growth-rate, which is subject to considerable uncertainty, is the growth-rate planned by management: in order to arrive at its valuation, the stock exchange applies a basic price/dividend multiple of b_1 to the *current* dividend, adding to this multiple the amount $b_2/100$ for every percentage point of expected *growth* of the dividend which latter, in a steady-state model, is the same as the expected growth-rate of the firm. All data are normalised by assets and in understanding the basic equations which follow, it should be appreciated that because all growth is internally financed, the current dividend per dollar of assets is precisely equal to earnings per dollar of assets less the growth rate, g, itself; since g, in effect, is investment per dollar of assets.

$$d = \hat{p} - ag - g \tag{1}$$

$$v = d.(b_1 + b_2 g) = (\hat{p} - ag - g)(b_1 + b_2 g). \tag{2}$$

From these, it follows that

$$g(\text{Max } v) = 1/2(\hat{p}/(1+a) - b_1/b_2); \tag{3}$$

and that

$$g(\text{Max } g, \text{ subject to } v \geq \hat{p}b_1) = 2g(\text{Max } v); \tag{4}$$

and in general that

$$g^* = M.(p/(1+a) - b_1/b_2). \tag{5}$$

Where

d = current dividend per dollar of assets,
v = stock-exchange value per ditto (the 'valuation ratio'),
$\hat{p}$ = operating profit rate,
g = steady-state growth rate of assets,
a = coefficient of costs of growth,
b_1 = price-dividend multiple for a non-growing firm,
b_2 = growth-enhancement factor,
M = motivational index ($1/2 \leq M \geq 1$),
g^* = optimum growth-rate for given M.

Now consider a large population of firms, all of whom are governed by the above model. From the various *caprices* of commercial history, ownership structure and owner motivation, they are all endowed with differing values of a, $\hat{p}$ and M. Furthermore, their individual values of these factors change from time to time in a somewhat random fashion. In order to simplify the investigation of the manifest effects of such variations, we proceed as follows. First assume that for all firms from 1 ... i ... n there is an individual coefficient of relative operating efficiency, such that

$$p_i = e_i \bar{p} \tag{6}$$

where $\hat{p}$ signifies the mean of all the $\hat{p}_i$. Then define a composite coefficient F_i, defined as

$$F_i = M_i e_i / (1 + a_i) \tag{7}$$

From which it follows that we may now write

$$g^*_i = F_i \bar{p} - M_i \frac{b_1}{b_2} \tag{8}$$

We now assume a stochastic process in which, starting from some initial point in time, each firm grows according to its own value of Equation (8). Then, after a time, eg after one year or some years, the cards are re-dealt and each firm acquires a new value of F_i. These new F_i may or may not be distributed independently of previous growth-rates. Because we are concerned with the relative development of large and small firms, we may express this problem by saying that after each deal we will regress the F_i in cross section on some measure, eg net assets, of the existing sizes of the firms. Express the resulting regression equation,

$$F_i = \gamma K_i + u_i \tag{9}$$

The value of γ may be or may not be significantly different from zero; if it *is* significantly different from zero, because of the complexity of the factors involved (and of the elusive character of previous empirical results on the relationship between the performance of firms and their size), we have no *a priori* prediction of the sign. But if the sign should prove negative, we shall speak of *Regression* (thus using the term in Galton's original sense); when it is positive we speak of *Anti-Regression*. The case where γ is zero is the case investigated by Gibrat, by Hart and Prais and by Simon and Bonini and by many others. So this case we shall call *Gibratesque*.

Combined effects of internal growth and major mergers

It will be assumed that it is legitimate simply to add the concentrating effects of mergers, as expressed by m, to the equations for the stochastic process of internal growth. The resulting equations are as follows:

(i)   *Gibratesque Case* ($\gamma = 0$)

$$_{o}X^2{}_t = t.(m + \bar{p}^2 o^2 u) \tag{10}$$

$$d\,_{o}X^2{}_t/dt = (m + \bar{p}^2 ou^2) \tag{11}$$

(ii)   *Other Cases* ($\gamma \neq 0$)

$$_{o}X^2{}_t = (m + \bar{p}^2 ou^2)(1 - (1 + \gamma\bar{p})^{2\,t})/(1 - (1 + \gamma\bar{p})) \tag{12}$$

$$d\,_{o}X^2{}_t/dt = (m + \bar{p}^2 o^2{}_u)1 + \bar{p})^{2\,(t-1)} \tag{13}$$

Thus, in the Gibratesque case, we have the familiar result that concentration increases persistently at a constant rate through time, while in the case of Regression the process is damped; in the case of Anti-Regression it is explosive. In the more familiar presentation of the Gibratesque case, mergers are not explicitly taken into account and the linear growth-rate of the variance of the logs of size is the variance of the growth-rates of the individual firms. In the present model we have added something for the effects of mergers and also expressed the variance of internal growth rates as the product, $\bar{p}^2 o^2 u$, derived from our explicit model of internal growth. Simulated time paths of concentration, based on empirically plausible values of the variables, are exhibited in Appendix 2, Chart 1.

Policy

If society objects to business concentration, it cannot depend on any reliable evidence of persistent Regression; that is to say, we have no robust evidence that firms of below-average logarithmic size tend to be more growth-motivated, more technologically and commercially dynamic and/or of above-average operating efficiency. For example, General Motors is noted for its technological conservatism and superior operating efficiency. And General Motors, except for the influence of the anti-trust laws, has certainly shown no disposition to disfavour growth.

Therefore, society should assume that it is faced with either Gibrat or Anti-Regression: Gibrat, as it were, is the null hypothesis.

Therefore, society's intervention should consist of discouraging mergers and/or of 'artificially' stimulating Regression. For the reasons already mentioned, this is by no means necessarily consistent with a policy which concentrates attention on the smallest size class, although the smallest size class would benefit incidentally.

The handicaps of small firms are intrinsic, but also relative; a firm that is now considered small would have been considered large in the Middle Ages. The most outstanding handicaps are those of diseconomies of small-scale management and the problems of finance. Some of the management problems are 'negotiable', especially since the advent of first degrees in business administration and of cheap but complex desk calculators. However, to the extent that we want small firms to be labour intensive (so that many people may enjoy being both beautiful and small) it remains the case that a desirable small firm may face a serious problem of personnel management, a problem which cannot easily be delegated and is the cause of the downfall of many. On the other hand, to the extent that it is precisely the intimacy and 'personalness' of the small firm that makes it desirable to society, many small firms do not, in fact, experience such difficulties. It follows that a degree of firmness, humanity and good sense represent one, but unfortunately only one, essential ingredient of the successful small entrepreneurship. It is an ingredient that is not easily taught in college.

The financial problems of the small firm arise because the goodwill is intangible, the risks locked in the mind and determination of the entrepreneur and the survival rate (as against the expected average rate of return) is low. The small-sized sector is characterised by unusually high birth rates and death rates, therefore presenting a classic problem for conservative bankers. Small firms must, therefore, grow mainly through internal finance. This handicap, however, requires some logical questioning because, in practice, a large proportion of the growth of large and medium firms is also internally financed. However, to the extent that large firms can establish quite significant steady-state debt-to-assets ratios at reasonable rates of interest, where small firms cannot, and to the extent that such reasonable rates of interest are significantly below average large-firm internal rates of operating profit, their optimum growth rates in a steady-state growth model, modified appropriately to take account of external finance, will be significantly enhanced. This is a possible cause of Auto-Regression that has not been included in our algebra: there is, of course, a fair amount of empirical evidence that large firms can borrow more cheaply than small firms. In order to investigate the effect of encouraging small firms, the simulation model already described not only assumed a significant rate of new entry into the smallest size class (in this we followed Simon and Ijiri *AER*, 1964, but our treatment of mergers is rather different from that of Simon and Ijiri *JPE*, 1971), but also that a significant proportion of these new entrants would survive through at least one year. The smallest size class was therefore constantly added to, this effect offsetting the otherwise persistent depletion due to the merger process. In each one-year period these surviving new entrants typically represented about 5% of the total number of firms. The general effect was to convert what had originally been a very slightly concentrated log-normal distribution into a distribution which was more or less J-shaped under the semi-log transform and more or less Pareto shaped under the double log transform (eg Simon and Ijiri, 1971).

The implications, for the 'sociological' character of the distribution, of the new-entry assumptions are not uninteresting. On the assumption that economic activity in the smallest size class was no more labour intensive than in other size classes, the proportion of total employment in the smallest size class at the beginning of the process, given the numbers assumed, would have been 3%. At the end of the process, ie fifteen years later, this figure would have been just over 10% (and the intermediate rate of change appeared more or less constant). Had the process also been associated with an increasing propensity to relative labour intensity among the smallest size class, this rate of growth of its proportion of employment could have been increased, perhaps, from approximately one-half of 1% per annum to as much as one per cent per annum. This would not, however, have prevented the proportion of employment among the largest size classes from also increasing; in effect, the employment distribution would have become bi-modal. Nor would the process have represented any amelioration of the growth of overall concentration as measured by output or assets.

Nevertheless, from the sociological point of view, the results of the entry assumptions are suggestive. In fact, in most countries, if we are prepared to include very small commercial units in our data, we already tend, I believe, to have the kind of bi-modal employment distribution that the experiment would have produced had it contained realistic assumptions about relative labour intensities of different size classes. Of course, there remains the perennial question of whether, from the point of view of small-firms policy, a firm that employs a few people to produce a lot of output should be regarded as 'large' or 'small'. The President of the World Bank (see his 1976 address to the Bank-Fund meetings) is clear about the answer: such a firm is not 'small' because it does not contribute to the social problems of employment or income distribution in developing countries. In non-stagnating, affluent societies without really serious non-Keynesian employment problems, whose interest in small firms stems from the ideas of the late Fritz Schumacher, the answer is not so obvious.

Appendix 1

P$_j$ matrix for major merger simulations

N.B. the figures are based on the hypothesis that elements are distributed normally down columns, truncated at size class 1

Size Classes	1	2	3	4	5	6			
1	0.0	2.5	4.0	2.5	0.5	0.0			
2	0.0	0.5	2.5	4.0	2.5	0.5	0.0		
3		0.0	0.5	2.5	4.0	2.5	0.5	0.0	
4			0.0	2.5	2.5	4.0	2.5	0.5	0.0

ETC.

NOTE: The elements represent the probabilities that firms of sizes indicated in the columns will acquire one firm of size indicated in rows; size class being logarithmic.

Appendix 2

CHART 1

Simulated path of logarithmic variance and concentration ratio on alternative assumptions relating to Regression and Anti-Regression

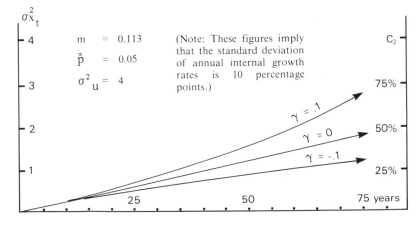

$\sigma\tilde{x}^2_t$

- 4   m   = 0.113   (Note: These figures imply
                                 that the standard deviation
          $\bar{\tilde{p}}$ = 0.05   of annual internal growth
- 3 σ^2_u = 4   rates is 10 percentage
                                 points.)

C_2

75%

- 2 $\gamma = .1$ 50%

- 1 $\gamma = 0$ 25%

        $\gamma = -.1$

        25   50   75 years

CHAPTER 5

Company finance in Europe – the impact on small firms

J. M. Samuels

It has been shown that the manufacturing and commercial sector in the UK has proportionately more large enterprises and proportionately fewer small enterprises than the equivalent sectors in the other major European industrial nations.[1] Britain finds itself in this position at a time when the older industrial nations are being challenged by the newer industrial nations of the Far East and South America. Certain industries, to be successful, need large enterprises to obtain the benefits from large-scale production, but it is precisely these industries that the newer industrial nations are developing. These newer industrial nations can combine the advantages of size with relatively low wage costs. Unfortunately, for many years smaller businesses were not encouraged in Britain – in fact they were discouraged – and so we find ourselves with an industrial structure which has many large units which are inflexible, and few new enterprises. We have been reluctant to allow the older industries to contract when faced with severe competition, because they usually consist of a few large corporations that are large employers of labour. We do not have enough small companies growing up to develop new ideas and new markets. It is only when we have a healthy small business sector that we will be able to handle the structural employment problem.

Why is the UK a nation of relatively large-scale businesses? Undoubtedly there are a number of reasons. This chapter will concentrate on just one of them, namely the financial. It will look at the way in which the financial system of a country can influence the size distribution of companies, and will suggest that the system in the UK is less helpful to smaller businesses than the system in most other European countries. This difference in the treatment of smaller businesses is due to past developments, to attitudes which have grown up over time, and to more recent political decisions.

Section I is comparative. It considers the reasons for the variation between countries in the methods they have adopted to finance their corporate sectors. No financial system is static, however, and in all countries changes are taking place in the way in which funds flow between sectors. In Section II we look at changes that have been taking place in the provision of finance for companies in the UK and at the implication of these changes for the smaller business.

I   Comparative company finance

The countries of Europe, industrialised at different times, have been influenced in different ways by historical events, have developed different social and political institutions, and are populated by people who show a variety of character and attitudes. It is not surprising, therefore, that the financial institutions and the methods of financing industry have varied from country to country. The European Economic Community is comparatively new, and the moves to introduce uniformity within the financial and monetary sectors of European countries have only just begun.

It is an opportune time to ask questions about the financial systems because, with the countries of the EEC beginning to move closer together in financial terms, the question of harmonisation of parts of the systems will arise. If past differences have had any significant effect in the development of sections of an economy, steps could be taken to ensure the distortion does not continue. Europe will have to make changes to face the growing competition from the newer industrial nations. Within Europe, Britain will have to make changes just to ensure she is not at a disadvantage compared with other member countries.

The financial institutions that exist in a country, their objectives and attitudes, are a result of the historical development of that country. It is the institutional structure of the money and capital markets that set a framework in which an individual company has to operate.[2]

To illustrate the different approaches, we will compare the methods of financing industry in West Germany and in the United Kingdom. There are two main differences. One arises over the involvement of the banks in the equity capital of companies and, consequently, in the control of companies. The other difference is in the levels of gearing that exist in the two countries and in the nature of the borrowed funds.

West Germany

The relationship between a company and its bankers has traditionally been much closer in West Germany than in the UK. The reasons for this different relationship are historic. Germany developed as an industrial power very much later than Britain and it was not possible for its financial system to evolve in the same way. Germany had to find a new way of financing its industrial development. British industry was able to gain its position of economic power through individual private enterprise, through the steady growth of smaller businesses. In fact, the British joint stock bank evolved at a comparatively late stage of the development, as did the principle of limited liability. German industrialisation, especially the growth of heavy industries, did not grow fast until after the Franco-Prussian war and almost immediately the system of equity capital with limited liability was introduced. Germany, at the time it industrialised, did not have the financial resources of Britain and so, in raising the enormous amount of capital required for investment in its heavy industries, it had to adopt borrowing and lending policies which would have been regarded in Britain as extremely risky. To progress to a highly industrialised state required a spirit of speculation. The establishment of the German banks and the principles that governed their lending policies contradicted most of the practice and principles that British banks had evolved in their role as providers of finance for international traders. Germany, wishing to grow quickly, had to create its own system.

From the beginning of industrialisation German banks have been the main financiers of German industry. The banks themselves built up the stock exchange business, often purchased the shares of the companies, and often accepted speculative securities as collateral for loans. The banks were once described as 'deposit speculative banks'. Creditors and debtors were exposed to greater risks than would have been considered acceptable in the UK. It was possible for the banks to dominate the money and capital markets from the very early days. In order to compete with the Anglo-Saxon world, Germany could not afford to have a small and unorganised banking system.

The combination of deposit banking and speculative investment in the German banking institutions sprang from the principle of the freedom of banks proclaimed in the middle of the 19th century. This meant that there were no restrictions placed on the investment policies of the banks. To meet the demand for credit from industry which greatly exceeded the amount of capital at the banks' disposal, deposits had to be raised from the public. Such deposits were attracted into the deposit banks, the co-operative credit institutions and the savings banks. From the earliest days banks helped sell and distribute the shares and debentures of the companies which they helped to finance. They could thus exert influence over the companies to whom they lent money and whose shares they distributed. The bank, knowing who owned a particular company's shares, could try to obtain the right to use the proxy vote of the shareholder at times of important decisions.

It was recognised that there were many dangers in the German system. The banks often became locked in with the companies to which they supplied money. If a company was in difficulties the bank may have had to continue to support it or lose its original investment. There were many crises in the German economy and the close relationship between banks and industry made the banks themselves feel the immediate effect of a down-turn in economic activity. Nevertheless, the German banking system from 1850 to 1914 was successful in meeting the needs of Germany. The soundness of the banking principles adopted in Great Britain could not be followed, simply because the financial resources were not available in Germany to allow for the levels of cover and security required, and more speculative procedures were unavoidable.

All this is history. What matters today is whether the system that evolved in Germany offers lessons which are useful to today's modern industrial societies; and if certain of the policies and practices of German banking give its industry advantages over the British system. An advantage of this close relationship between a bank and the company is the exact knowledge the bank has of its client, of its management and of the future potential of the company. For the bank, this means greater security in that it knows how its investment is being handled, and for the company, the advantage of expert advice and a financially powerful shareholder or bondholder who can supply funds for future needs.

The extent to which the bank can interfere with the management of the company may depend upon the size of the company. West German bankers are keen to point out that the banks do not, and could not, control the large companies. The big companies use more than one bank and are in a position to 'shop around' banks.

Where, however, a company is of small or medium size, a bank is in a very powerful position. A bank with a large enough shareholding could, in the last resort, get rid of the management. Banks have special departments whose job is to co-operate with the companies in which they invest and keep themselves informed as to whether the company is succeeding, as well as to offer expert advice where this is felt to be needed.

Many people are of the opinion that German banks interfere too much and that it is not the proper function of a bank to become involved in giving advice on the running of the business. However, there are situations in the UK where banks have found it necessary to interfere to protect their investments; for example, Rolls-Royce and BSA – and there are many shareholders of these companies who wish the banks had acted more quickly.

Because the West German banks have in the past been more

willing to take risks than the British banks, they have been more willing to lend to smaller businesses and to newer enterprises. They had to take risks to help the country industrialise quickly, whereas British banks and other financial institutions could avoid riskier types of enterprise. The West German banks, with a closer working relationship with their customers, were in a better position to be able to judge new developments. The British banks, wishing to maintain an arm's length relationship, were not in a position to assess whether new ideas were worth backing. They were not in the venture capital market, yet only they and the other financial institutions had the necessary funds.

Another difference in methods of financing is that, traditionally, in West Germany the levels of gearing (leverage) have been higher.[3] This means that a company in West Germany has, over time, been able to obtain a higher proportion of the finance it requires from borrowing than has a company in the UK. It must be said, however, that these differences are becoming less; the British banks in the 1970s responded to the need for increased funds to finance working capital. One major difference that has remained is that borrowings in the UK are mainly of a short-term, bank overdraft nature, whereas in West Germany the banks are more willing to lend medium and long. In 1975, for example, 16.9% of the sources of funds for West German enterprises was provided by medium to long-term bank loans, whereas in the UK, in that year only, in the region of 5% of total funds was medium- to long-term borrowing. More recently, however, banks and other financial intermediaries in the UK have become more willing to lend long.

The difference in the level of borrowings and in the terms is important, as it is the smaller company that is more dependent on borrowing, particularly from the banks, so the smaller companies in the UK have been at a disadvantage, not finding it as easy as smaller companies in West Germany, or larger companies in their own country, to obtain finance for long-term investments.

Not all financing methods pursued in West Germany would be welcome in Britain. The dominant role of the banks, both with regard to shares and to borrowing, would be considered dangerous. However, the more independent system that exists in the UK has a cost, and we should recognise that to have an arm's length relationship between banks, insurance companies, pension funds and industrial companies, means that there is less willingness to invest long-term. The cost of capital is higher in the UK than in West Germany and many other European countries.

At least two changes would be necessary before the cost of capital could be reduced in the UK. The first is an increase in the level of gearing that is considered acceptable, meaning that banks would have to accept lower levels of asset and interest cover on the loans they make available to companies. The second change would be that the financial institutions provide more long-term loans, and accept that their own long-term interests are tied in with the success of British industry. The change in the level of gearing would also mean that, in return for an increasing bank or other institutional commitment to the companies, the existing boards would have to share some of their power, and be willing to accept intervention and representation from the banks. And those companies not wishing to do so might find their competitors would have more funds at lower cost and consequently more profitable investment opportunities and more machinery per employee.

France

In France it is the position of the state-owned banks that distinguishes the French financial system from that of most other European countries. The three largest commercial banks are publicly owned, as are three of the biggest insurance companies. The public and semi-public financial institutions handle about 85% of total bank deposits, giving the French government tremendous influence over the funds available to finance investment.

One question that puzzles observers of France is how a market economy, where everyone is to some extent free to make their own decisions, can still have an economic plan that works. It is, in fact, an 'indicative' plan. The government, by approving the plans, takes on the responsibility of attempting to direct the economy according to the plan, to induce and persuade industry to take actions which conform to the plan. It gives individuals and businesses a financial inducement which it hopes will be sufficient to persuade them to make the 'right' decisions. Where the government owns the industry it can, of course, direct investment to where it believes it will achieve the best results. Also, as the largest purchaser of the products of many industries, it can favour those companies that make decisions that conform to the plan. It can, as can all governments, adjust its tax and monetary policies in an attempt to achieve results that fit in with the plan.

The French government exercises certain controls over banks and capital issues; and because of this it has a considerable influence over the borrowing of private business. For example, the *Credit National*, a state-controlled institution which at one time granted more than 90% of all loans made to private firms for capital construction and equipment, will not grant credit of more than a certain figure unless the borrower can show that his use of the funds fits in with the national plan. If you control the supply of funds to companies, it is fairly easy to ensure that their investments conform to the plan. It is also easy to ensure that small businesses obtain a fair share of the funds.

The French government exercises a considerable influence on the decisions of French industry; it does this more by control of finance and financial incentives and inducements than by direct authoritarian controls. The financial incentives usually take the form of subsidies. For example, if it is thought necessary for a certain industry to modernise its equipment, the government can help reduce the tax bill of companies in that industry, by allowing a rapid rate of depreciation on the new investments. Similarly, if it was thought desirable to develop a certain region of the country, the government could either grant subsidies, place orders with the companies in the region, or offer lower taxes to firms that invest in that region. If it wished to encourage new firms or small firms, it could channel funds to them. The government has even gone as far as to guarantee interest payments on loans granted to private companies, if the securities in question were issued to obtain funds for top priority projects.

The plan provides the French government with a view of the choices open to them. The committee that is responsible for finance for industry tries to spot any bottlenecks, any shortages of investment in sectors that are vital to the economy and any differences between the funds available and the investment plans of industry. It was in France that the imaginative form of business co-operation, GIEs (Economic Interest Groups) were developed, which have particularly helped small firms. There are aspects of the French system which would not be acceptable in Britain, in particular the nationalisation of large parts of the financial sector and the extent of government interference in the private sector of industry.

It is an interesting question whether the French economy could have grown as quickly as it has done without the channelling of savings into planned investments. France does not have such a well developed capital market as Britain and it has not traditionally had banks with such close involvement with industry as in Germany. It is doubtful, therefore, whether the savings in France, even if large enough, would have found their way into the most productive long-run investment opportunities without the indicative planning system the country adopted. As in the UK, the funds might have found their way into the companies that could show the greatest short-term gains and it could have taken a long time before the French developed close patterns of ownership and control between banks and companies.

II   Problems in provision of finance for small companies

1. The trends in the provision of finance in the UK have worked against small companies. Savings were once undertaken by a comparatively small number of people in a society, and they tended to invest in companies they knew. The proportion of the total savings of a country in the hands of such individuals has been falling steadily over time.[4] There has been a trend in most countries towards saving through contractual savings schemes and it has been particularly dramatic in the UK. There are many reasons for this shift, one of which is the tax advantage. If an individual saves and then uses his savings to buy shares in a company, or to loan money to a company, he is investing after-tax income. He has earned income, he has paid tax and what is left over he is free to invest. If, however, he has to pay part of his salary into a pension scheme, the money being invested on his behalf by the pension fund is the gross amount deducted; it has not been subject to a tax deduction. If the individual places his savings into an insurance policy, he is allowed to claim partial tax relief on the premiums.

This discouraging of direct investment applies to the stocks and shares of both large and small businesses. It hurts the small business more, however, because the financial intermediaries that are now the recipients of the savings have been less willing to invest in small companies than would the private individual investing directly. There are even more discouragements to investments in the British tax system, namely capital gains tax, the taxation of companies and capital transfer tax. These forms of taxation have particularly harmed smaller businesses.

2. British governments have encouraged saving to move to areas other than industry. For many years, central and local government have been big borrowers in the capital and money markets. They have been competing for the same funds as industry and they are less conscious of the cost of that money than a business that has to earn a profit. As borrowers, they have helped force up the interest rates.

3. The savings have not been flowing directly from the saver to the company, particularly not the smaller company. The savings rate in the UK has, however, shown a considerable increase in recent years and the funds have been channelled to the financial intermediaries. We need now to consider why the smaller business has not received an appropriate share of these funds. Institutions have shown a preference for investing in the larger enterprise. There are economies of scale when purchasing shares. The administrative costs of

purchasing 10,000 shares in one company are less than the administrative cost of purchasing 1,000 shares in each of 10 companies.

The institutions wish to be able to sell a block of shares whenever they feel it necessary, without disturbing the price of that share by more than a few pennies. To do this, they need to be investing in large companies. In small companies they could well be selling a significant proportion of the total shares of that company and so be disturbing the share price.

The risks attached to investing in large companies are less than those involved in investing in small companies. The amount of information known about a large company is usually considerable and the institutional investor can assess the risks, whereas with a small company, the available information is often insufficient. The small company is usually less diversified, and is so less able to withstand trade fluctuations. Because of the higher risks when funds are made available to smaller firms, it is usually at a higher cost. The small company, therefore, needs to earn higher returns than the large company before an investment breaks even.

4. One source of external finance is the Stock Exchange. A quotation can, however, be expensive for a small company. In fact an over the counter market has developed in the UK which should benefit smaller companies. It is similar in idea to markets that have existed in Germany, USA and other countries for many years. It enables a company of smaller to medium size to obtain the advantages of having a market develop in its shares without having to meet the cost and administrative requirements of a full market quotation.

Smaller companies in the UK have suffered relative to their counterparts in other European countries, such as Germany and France, from the absence of an active long-term loan market, a debenture market. The market for corporate securities is not well developed in the UK and so the smaller company has been deprived of yet another source of possible funds.

The large company has access to markets that the smaller company cannot approach. We now have large international markets, the Euro-currency and Euro-bond markets. A large company with a proven record does not have to rely on national money or capital markets; monetary restrictions and pressure on interest rates at home need not deter it from seeking funds outside the country. This path is clearly not open to the smaller company.

5. What of internal finance? Here again the smaller firm has been discriminated against, in the matter of self financing. Close company legislation means that the smaller company has been taxed as if it distributed a certain proportion of its net earnings whether or not it

has in fact done so. Such companies are not able to keep a high proportion of their profits in the business. They can distribute the profits as dividends, in which case the dividends will be taxed at the marginal tax of the receiving shareholder, or the company can retain the funds and pay the shareholder's higher income tax rates on the profits. There has in the past been little incentive offered through the tax system to the smaller business. It is appreciated that this legislation was introduced in an attempt to bring equity into the tax system, but one effect has been to discourage initiative.

6. Fortunately, one of the trends leading to a decline in the number of smaller companies has shown a slowing down, namely the merger and takeover movement. This occurred in most European countries in the late 1960s and early 1970s but was particularly strong in the UK. In the period from 1964 to 1971 the average quoted company in the UK relied more heavily on growth by merger than on net new investment in fixed assets.[5] It was usually the smaller company being absorbed by the larger and the most active acquirers were doubling their size every two years. It has been shown that these mergers did nothing to improve the economic performance of the country, and in fact did nothing to improve the profitability and returns for the shareholders of the continuing companies. There were, of course, many examples of handsome capital gains for the selling shareholders. Although mergers and takeovers are now not such an important issue, there is always a danger that this type of financial activity could increase again, with the smaller company as the victim. In fact one reason why companies merged was to become larger and so be less likely to be the victims of an unwanted takeover, rather than with any idea of improving performance.

III   Present trends in Britain

Financial institutions have in the last few years introduced a number of imaginative schemes to help the smaller firm. Some banks are going out of their way to lend to smaller businesses and some institutions are now more willing to buy securities from private businesses. However, because of previous bad experiences in the provision of venture capital and because of administrative costs, some institutions will only consider proposals from the larger private businesses, those seeking funds in excess of £100,000.

In the past there was no need for British financial institutions to take risks – money was flowing to the smaller newer businesses from other sources. Now a change in approach is required. Funds need to be provided where the levels of risk are greater than that previously considered to be the acceptable limit. The loan needs to be judged not on the basis of a non-existent or inadequate financial record of the business, but on the strength of the individuals involved and the prospects for the markets they are in: an assessment based more on potential than past performance.

The British government now helps by providing guarantees to banks lending to small business, through the Loan Guarantee Scheme. This was introduced in 1981, and thus came later than similar provisions in other countries such as Germany and the United States, which had the government-backed Small Business Investment Scheme.

Over recent years institutional shareholders in Britain have been net purchasers of company securities and private individuals net sellers. The combined institutions held 26.6% of the total quoted shares in 1966 and this had increased to 43% in 1975. They are increasing their holdings by about 1.5% of the total equity market per annum.[6] Even though institutions have shown a preference for holdings in the largest companies, the proportion of shares held by them has increased for all size groups of companies, the large, medium and small quoted companies.

Is the concentration of share ownership into the hands of a few institutions a cause for concern? It is possible to argue either way. The institutions obtain most of their funds from comparatively small savers. Individuals contribute to pension schemes, pay life insurance premiums, and buy unit trusts, and the funds that pass into the hands of the financial institutions are used to buy shares. So it can be argued that now, instead of a few wealthy people owning shares, a large number of individuals are, through financial intermediaries, involved in share ownership. The returns from equity ownership will not go to the few wealthy individuals but to the pension fund contributors and insurance company policy holders.

However, the individuals who through their savings give the buying power to the insurance companies and pension funds have very little say in the way their investments are handled. It is the managers of the pension funds and the insurance companies who have power. It is they who decide to buy a share, when to sell it, whether to subscribe to a new issue, whether to invest in small businesses, and in new businesses, whether to support a takeover, and on rare occasions whether or not to remove a company's directors.

In fact the institutional shareholders have shown a very strong wish to maintain an arm's length relationship with the companies in which they invest and have not been inclined to become involved in the management of them. In West Germany where the banks have become closely involved in decision making within companies, they have been heavily criticised politically for using their power in this way. Politically it may be wise of the British institutions to avoid this form of criticism, but it has not meant that they have been free from threats of nationalisation and it has left British companies ill supplied with long-term finance.

One other worry about present trends, beyond the concentration of funds available for investment into a few hands, is the concentration within industry itself. It is important to appreciate that even if there were no economies of scale and no advantages in the provision of finance there would still be an increase in concentration over time. If all sized companies have the same probability of growing at any particular rate, there will still be a tendency for concentration to increase. With economies of scale and easier access to finance operating on top of this neutral process, then there will be even faster increases in the rate of concentration.

Prais and others have shown where the present trends will lead if nothing is done to change the existing arrangements. It is important to appreciate that up to now this increase in concentration of industry in the hands of large firms has not led to an improvement in the competitiveness of the British economy, but rather to a decrease. We now need to encourage small companies, to stimulate inventiveness and initiative.

If the smaller company is to be encouraged, it will need more help with the provision of finance than it has obtained in the past. The government may have to help even more, and the extent to which it needs to become involved depends on the willingness of the banks and financial institutions to respond. The major banks already have contacts and working relationships with smaller business. It is the pension funds and insurance companies that should be encouraged to invest an increasing proportion of their vast funds in the newer business and the smaller business.

References

1. See, in addition to George and Ward, Prais and the Bolton Report quoted in Chapters 1–3; Walshe, G., *Recent trends in monopoly in Great Britain,* Cambridge University Press, 1974; Bannock, G., *The Juggernauts,* Weidenfeld and Nicholson, 1971 and *The smaller business in Britain and Germany,* Walton, 1976.

2   Samuels, J. M., Groves, R. E. V. and Goddard, S., *Company finance in Europe,* Institute of Chartered Accountants, 1976.

3.   Coates, J. H. and Woolley, P. K., 'Corporate gearing in the EEC', *Journal of Business Finance and Accounting,* Spring 1975; National Economic Development Office, *Finance for investment, a study of methods available for financing investment,* London, 1975.

4.   *Royal Commission on the distribution of income and wealth* (the Diamond Commission), HMSO, 1975; Samuels, J. M. and McMahun, P. C., *Saving and investment in the U.K. and W. Germany,* Wilton, 1978.

5.   Meeks, G., *Disappointing marriage: a study of the gains from merger,* Cambridge University Press, 1977; Singh, A., *Takeovers, their relevance to the stock market and the theory of the firm,* Cambridge University Press, 1971; Walshe, G., *op cit.*

6.   Moyle, J., *The pattern of ordinary share ownership 1950-1979,* Cambridge University Press, 1971; Briston, R. J. and Dobbins, *The institutional shareholder,* Institute of Chartered Accountants, London, 1978.

CHAPTER 6

Small firms and the German economic miracle

Willibrord Sauer

Introduction

The astonishing economic recovery of West Germany after World War II is generally attributed to the re-emergence of German big business. Krupp, Thyssen and Bayer are three of the most striking examples. Although small and medium enterprises make up more than 95% of Germany's businesses, their contribution is generally overlooked.[1]

The importance of small firms is to be measured not only by their direct contribution to the gross national product, but also by their direct and indirect contribution to the productive efficiency of bigger firms in their role as competitors and sub-contractors and to the overall efficiency of the economy. In addition, they have played a profoundly important role in the stability of post-war German society, dependent as it has been on a free market economy. The situation of small businesses in pre-war Germany was very unfavourable and this contributed much to the unstable economic and social conditions of the time. Recognition of this accounts, in part, for the great attention they received in the post-war recovery plans of West Germany.

Crucial in the rapid and general recovery of Germany's economy were, of course, the political decisions that were taken by the Western Allies, particularly the United States – for example, in the launching of the European Recovery Programme. Second only to these were the roles of Germany's own post-war political leaders, notably Chancellor Adenauer and his Minister of Economics, Professor L. Erhard. If miracle there was, and Professor Erhard maintains that in Germany's economic recovery there was not,[2] it is to be seen in the concourse of vital political decisions then taken by all those involved.

The social market economy

Professor Erhard's policies were based upon a clear political philosophy. The primary aim was to prevent the re-emergence of old class differences arising out of income disparities. He fought for an economic system which would bring ever increasing purchasing power to all. High priority was given to avoiding economic cycles by emphasising steady growth and the expansion of employment, high productivity and increases in incomes in line with output per head. He concentrated upon furthering competition as the most efficient means of achieving and maintaining prosperity for all.[3]

Competition is only possible if there are a sufficient number of firms in the market and Professor Erhard's first aim was to encourage as many people as possible to start up businesses. New business formation was therefore facilitated. Restrictions upon trade were abolished and a strict anti-trust policy followed. This meant ignoring demands for policies favouring the large scale industries in which pre-war Germany had excelled.

Equally, in spite of demands to the contrary, especially from the distributive trades,[4] Erhard never pursued a policy of protecting small firms from the healthy rigours of competition. Protection would only lead to inefficiency. But he also took great care that general government measures did not give any direct or indirect advantage to large firms. Given the crucial role of small firms in the social market economy, their viability had to be taken into account in all fields of government policy (including regional, urban, fiscal and social policies). Non-interventionist and non-selective industrial policies together with price stability and continuous economic growth provided a good climate for the creation and growth of small business.

Three measures, in particular, were enacted to make these policies effective. The first was that low interest rate loans were made available to those starting, modernising or expanding a small firm. Secondly, although strong anti-trust measures prevented the cartelisation of large firms, small firms were allowed to group together to compete against large firms. In this particular case, cartelisation increases the total amount of competition, rather than decreasing it.

Thirdly, in certain crafts and trades, the Basic Law on Skilled Crafts and Trades, 1953, required new entrants to hold proficiency certificates before they were allowed to practise. The effect of these standards on the quality of production and the efficiency of small firms was reinforced (as will be shown) by professional training and information services provided by trade associations of various kinds, most of which received financial assistance from the public sector. The scope of the scheme is demonstrated by the numbers involved. In 1981/2 there were 674,560 apprentices in training. Of this total, 224,094 took their final exams, with 86.6% passing. A further 37,372 adults, who were already qualified, took the 'master craftsman' exams, with a 75.8% success rate. This apprentice scheme is still entirely run by private firms, the state and local authority subsidising the education the apprentices receive on their one day a week technical school attendance and the 'skill centres' they attend for practical training.

It should be emphasised that the proficiency regulations are designed to promote quality and flexibility of performance in competing to meet consumer needs, not to act as a restriction upon trade. It is important to note that because it is not possible to start a business without qualifications, the government knows that any *handwerk* businesses receiving its aid will have a minimum standard of competence. Furthermore, although there is a small danger from centrally regulated proficiency standards, it prevents a more important problem from arising. In periods of high unemployment large numbers of unemployed enter the *handwerk* professions trading as a small business. They are only able to compete with established craftsmen on price. These newcomers, however, frequently go bankrupt, although they still damage the established trade by forcing lower prices – thus possibly causing well-qualified businessmen also to go bankrupt. The proficiency regulations described above help to prevent this from happening.

The distinctive nature of German policy

The nature of German policies is brought out clearly if they are compared with those of France. After World War II, the French government was committed to making economic and fiscal policies favourable to the success of bigger firms. At this time the French economy was dominated by agriculture with much of its industry serving agriculture, as in the processing of food products. The French government felt that it should promote industry so as to take the place which Germany had occupied. What the French government did was to create, almost exclusively, the conditions for the growth of big business. This is why France has today strong motor, aviation, computer and nuclear industries. The promotion of large firms in key sectors, however, was carried out at the expense of neglecting the interests of wage earners and the self-employed. This led to near revolution in 1968 and the neo-Poujadiste movements in 1972-73.

Four problems remain unsolved in the French economy. First, only some sectors are modernised, and they are dominated by very large firms. Second, the small firm sector is not fully integrated into the modern economy. Third, the position of the wage earner has not been resolved, in particular the issue of co-determination remains open. Fourth (and this applies to other European countries too) poor industrial relations have retarded industrial development.

In Germany the involvement of the trades unions in redeveloping and reconstructing the country was vital. So too was the guaranteeing of the rights and working conditions of workers in firms and enterprises. Many countries have not gone as far as Germany in these matters. The almost total destruction of Germany after the second World War forced German workers and owners to create an alliance in order to reconstruct and compete with the world. This is not simply my own view as a German; it was borne out by the Uri Report prepared for the European Community and published in 1973.[5] This report concluded that in the Community there were two types of economies:

1. Modern economies in which small firms were well integrated and as competitive and well equipped as the bigger firms. Germany, Belgium and the Netherlands came into this category.

2. Economies with very competitive and modern large firms and a large sector of uncompetitive small firms constituting a sort of medieval sub-economy. France and Italy were included in this second group.

It is not true that because Italy and France have more small firms than Germany conditions for small business must be more favourable in those countries. In fact, it is quite evident – for example in the South of Italy – that small firms make fine products but their proprietors quite often earn less than the national minimum wage. In France and more especially in Italy, there has always been more unemployment than in Germany and there are no regulations requiring craftsmen to be qualified before setting up in business or taking employment. There is a pronounced tendency during recessions for unemployed workers with some craft skills to register as craftsmen and either work or 'moonlight' for less than the accepted wage. When the economy is running well in Italy there are 850,000 to 900,000 craft firms; when the economy is depressed there are 1.2 to 1.4 million. A similar situation occurs in France where in bad times the number of enterprises goes up from the normal level of 750,000 to 950,000 or nearly a million. The additional cut-price competition creates even harsher conditions for craft trades leading to decreases in the total number of firms.

It is not wise for governments to give subsidies to assist unqualified people to set up new businesses. It exacerbates the problem because the newcomers can only compete on price and thus, eventually, cause more bankruptcies. That is why, belatedly, the French government is now insisting on minimum standards of management ability before assisting new businesses to start up.

In Germany, economic policy has not concentrated on the interests of large firms in key sectors at the expense of small firms. An educational policy paying special attention to vocational, on-the-job training has proved an absolute necessity. It is impossible to acquire the necessary professional skills and to develop the sense of initiative and responsiblity by training at school. If facilities for after-school training did not exist in Germany, it would have proved impossible to avoid a division in the national economy between efficient modern large firms and out of date, inefficient small ones.

In spite of the limited and secondary intervention by government, the inevitable trend towards further concentration has continued. The number of firms in the small business sector has declined by almost 50% while the number of people working in each enterprise has increased from an average of 2.5 per firm to 8.3 per firm in 1982. This trend is due to both increasing rationalisation and mechanisation The 60s and 70s saw fiscal and social legislation which favoured capital investment. This imposed considerable additional costs on the use of labour in the production process. Because *handwerk* firms employ larger than average proportions of labour, they have been adversely affected by these laws.

Handwerk
Number of enterprises

1950	886,500
1960	734,600
1970	585,100
1980	496,200
1981	495,200

The total turnover in 1982 was DM374.9 billion. Turnover per employee was DM91,700. There were 15,548 new *handwerk* businesses started in 1981/2 – but 18,220 exits (through close-down or bankruptcy).

Information and training services

There is a very strong and lively tradition in Germany of promoting and defending the interests of the self-employed. When the industrial revolution swept away the Guilds, the old notions of craft trades evolved into the modern concept of *handwerk*. In 1976, some 507,300 firms employing almost 4 million people were engaged in *handwerk*.[6] Businessmen in *handwerk* have set up an efficient network of local, regional and national bodies, called Chambers of Craft Industries and Trades (CIT), which look after their members' interests and provide specialised services.

The CIT also provide additional facilities for the vocational aspects of running apprenticeship schemes and on-the-job training, which neither the specialised small firm nor the schools could provide. There are CIT skill centres which are practice orientated and are known as *überbetriebliche Unterweisung*. A further function of the CIT is to run the apprentice, journeyman and master exams. CIT consists of special chambers of trade for skilled crafts and trades covered by the German *handwerk* definition. There are seven principal groups: construction; metal; wood; clothing; food; health (including chemical and mechanical cleaning); glass, ceramic and paper.

Other sectors of commerce and industry have similar organisations (chambers of trade and industry) giving small firms, with their middle-class orientation, special attention. Government support is given to these bodies and this is the policy of all political parties as reflected in a number of official reports on the situation of small and medium firms in recent years.[7]

The Chambers of Craft Industries and Skilled Trades are self-governing bodies with public status and are charged under law with the supervision of vocational training, the organisation of examinations and the granting of master diplomas (Class A occupations) and proficiency certificates (Class B occupations). They control and assist on-the-job vocational training, which is supplemented by one day a week obligatory courses for over 750,000 apprentices (end-1981) given at state technical schools. They have large skill centres in which they arrange additional practical training, organise examinations and run advanced technical and management courses. All the main skill centres run refresher courses for management and workers of member firms. They also teach new technologies, especially familiarity with computer techniques. They do this in a practical and often visual way, for example, by the use of models of machines, so that the courses appeal to tradesmen and craftsmen who are not accustomed to dealing in abstractions. Some of these courses are provided in the day time, some in the evening and there are many sandwich courses, some especially adapted for the older members with heavy responsibilities at their places of work.

There are some 42 Chambers of Craft Industry and Trades (CIT) in Germany, one in each large town; Cologne, for example, has 72,000 member firms, eight offices and divisions covering specialised trades such as plumbing, building and electrical work. The CIT provide the following services, in addition to training:

Information on local, urban and regional planning, firm location, environment safety and other regulations, markets and marketing, plant and premises, trade exhibitions, exports, etc;

Advice on setting up in business, labour law and other regulations, (including credit-guarantees), technical design and management problems;

Accountancy assistance, book-keeping services, some of them computerised, payroll systems, taxation, etc.

One of the most important tasks of the CIT is to represent and defend their members' interests vis-a-vis local, regional and federal authorities and other organisations. They also publish journals which keep their members up to date on knowledge useful to their craft and trade. The various divisions also collaborate in the publication of a twice-monthly newspaper with social, economic, fiscal and general information of special interest to small firms. The *Handwerk Presse* has a circulation of more than 500,000.

The cost of the services of the CIT is partly met by levies on their members, but Federal Government grants are available to pay between 60 and 80% of the cost of all information, instruction and advisory services. There are other organisations providing similar services for small firms outside *handwerk* and which also receive subsidies from government. The Chambers of Trade and Commerce are less specialised bodies providing services for a wide range of firms, including small firms for which there is a separate division. Others include the National Association for Retail Traders and Shop-keepers. This organisation advises retailers on shopfitting and window dressing, purchasing and credit and computerisation. Another is the National Federation of Hotel and Restaurant Businesses.

Financial facilities for small firms

The provision of credit on suitable and stable terms is an important element in German policies towards small businesses, and it remains primarily the banks' role to provide credit for them. Aid in providing low interest loans can be particularly effective in Germany, where there are a variety of financial institutions which are organised to provide credit for small firms. These institutions, particularly the Savings Banks, the Co-operative Banks and the Peoples Banks, in fact, provide much more finance for small firms than the commercial banks.

The Co-operative Banks were created in the late nineteenth century by men who observed that a large part of local savings were being channelled into large banks in the big cities and from there into large firms, and said to themselves 'We have got to stop this. The wealth created in towns and villages has got to stay there and be re-invested there'. As a complement to lending money these institutions provide specialised information services on market conditions and even on government or commercial contacts and sources of technical advice in which they work closely with the CIT.[8] The banks take pains to keep themselves informed about the markets in which their customers operate. These banks are in a better position to advise their customers and to assess requirements for loans than the large commercial banks which may be far away in the cities. For small firms, it is most important for there to be a network of small banks that are close to the reality of the market and the small firms' situation, so that the judgement of the banker is rooted in the actual place where the money is spent.

Although they understand particularly well the special problems and needs of small firms, the Savings Banks and the Popular Banks have to charge market rates for their deposits and their lending or they could not remain in business. At both the Federal and regional (Länder) levels of government, however, funds are available for low cost lending to small firms. Originally these funds largely came from Marshall Aid, some of the money being set aside for lending to small firms. As the loans were repaid they have been re-lent so that 30 years later the European Recovery Programme (ERP) is still benefiting German business. Loans provided for small and medium firms have been increased in recent years from DM300 million in 1974 to DM500 million in 1975 and to DM1.8 billion in 1981. DM860 million of this total went specifically to help business start-ups. The interest rate 'subsidy' is at the time of writing of the order of 2 to 2.5% and in Berlin and the area on the East German border it can be as much as 3%. This means that small firms will be paying perhaps 7 or 7.5% when the market rate of interest is 9.5 to 10%.

Some firms, especially those contemplating a major expansion, find that they cannot raise the necessary security for large loans. All banks have to comply with regulations governing their solvency and if they cannot secure their lending they must limit it. The solution to this problem in Germany (and in Austria and Switzerland) is the credit guarantee institution. These institutions were set up after World War II by the CIT in co-operation with the Savings, Co-operative and Popular banks. The government provided some of the necessary funds and underwrote 60% of the liabilities of the companies which took the form of private limited companies. The credit guarantee companies indemnify the banks for a proportion of the risk on loans which are accepted by them. The borrower applies to the credit guarantee company for the guarantee via his bank. After asking for and considering the advice of CIT, the credit guarantee company makes its decision. The loss experience on guarantees was very low – well under one per cent up to 1976. Since then, however, it has increased considerably, as a result of the adverse economic environment. It is now just under two per cent. This low failure rate has enabled the credit guarantee companies to build up substantial reserves and the underwriting of the government is now hardly necessary. In all, over the last 29 years the Guarantee Companies have handled more than 75,000 guarantees involving an average of about DM145,000 each. A particularly useful feature of the loan guarantee system is its 'multiplier' effect. This works because when the guarantee is made, the borrower is often then able to increase his normal rate of borrowing. In 1981 there were 4,133 loans, totalling DM601 million – although only DM463 million of this total was actually guaranteed.

Union attitudes

The unions in Germany prefer large firms. Unions are normally in favour of mergers and anything which will make firms larger. This is simply because it is easier to unionise large firms than small ones and it is easier to increase membership in large firms. In small firms the employees have direct access to the owner manager and thus feel the necessity to join a union less strongly. The impersonal nature of relationships between management and employees in a large firm encourages unionisation, and the pressures which unions can apply in large firms are greater.

Conclusion

While the Social Democrats were in power, their underlying encouragement to the trade unions led to high wage levels. This was accentuated by the economic boom. Furthermore, the additional costs of employing labour shot up. They are now 77% of the actual wage (in 1966 they were at 43% – for firms employing more than 50 people) as a result of such measures as health insurance, maternity leave, sick pay for up to six weeks' absence, and so on. It has become more attractive to too many people in Germany – and elsewhere – to be a wage earner rather than risk an entrepreneurial role. The new Kohl government is determined to change this trend and redress the balance in favour of entrepreneurial behaviour. The logic behind its thinking is that the welfare state can no longer finance itself.

Germany is returning to the principles and values that underlay the Erhard and Adenauer periods when the economics of the free and social market economy prevailed.

Bibliography

Verzeichnis allgemeiner Handwerkspublikationen

Handwerk 1981
Jahresbericht des Zentralverbandes des Deutschen Handwerks.
Herausgeber: ZDH, Johanniterstr. 1, 5300 Bonn, 1981, 412 S.

Bericht über die Lage des Handwerks im Jahre 1981
Herausgeber: Bundesministerium für Wirtschaft Villemobler Str. 76, 5300 Bonn, 1982, 45 S.

Das Handwerk
Herausgeber: Bundesministerium für Wirtschaft, Villemobler Str. 76, 5300 Bonn, 1981, 71 S.

Deutsches Handwerksblatt
Offizielles Organ des Zentralverbandes des Deutschen Handwerks, des Deutschen Handwerkskammertages und der Bundesvereinigung der Fachverbände des Deutschen Handwerks, Bekanntmachungsblatt der *Aktion Modernes Handwerk (AMH)*, Verein zur Förderung der Öffentlichkeitsarbeit des Handwerks, Bonn, Bekanntmachungsblatt der GHM-Gesellschaft für Handwerksausstellungen und - messen mbH, München.
Herausgeber: Zentralverband des Deutschen Handwerks, Johanniterstr. 1, 5300 Bonn.

Internationales Gewerbearchiv
der Klein- und Mittelbetriebe in der modernen Wirtschaft.
Herausgeber: Schweizerisches Institut für gewerbliche Wirtschaft an der Hochschule St. Gallen für Wirtschafts- und Sozialwissenschaften. Schriftleitung: Prof. Dr. A. Gutersohn, St. Gallen.

Junges Handwerk
Verlag Hans Holzmann, Gewerbestr. 2, 8939 Bad Wörishofen.

Schriftenreihe des Zentralverbandes des Deutschen Handwerks
Herausgeber: Zentralverband des Deutschen Handwerks, Johanniterstr. 1, 5300 Bonn.

Schriften zur Mittelstandsforschung
Herausgeber: Institut für Mittelstandsforschung, Maximilianstr., 20, 5300 Bonn.

Beiträge zur Mittelstandsforschung
Herausgeber: Institut für Mittelstandsforschung.

Informationen zür Mittelstandsforschung
Herausgeber: Institut für Mittelstandsforschung.

Reihe des Instituts für Handwerkswirtschaft
Forschungsinstitut des Deutschen Handwerksintituts Ottostr. 7/V, 8000 München.

Göttinger Handwerkswirtschaftliche Studien
Herausgeber: Seminar für Handwerkswesen an der Universität Göttingen, 3400 Göttingen.

References

1. A small firm is one with up to 49 employees. Medium-sized firms may be taken as those with 50–500 employees, but this general definition is not satisfactory for all sectors. See *Zur Problem situation mittleständischer betriebe*, Institut für Mittelständsforschung, Universität Köln, Verlag Otto Schwartz, Göttingen, 1976, pp. 1–30.
2. Professor L. Erhard, *Wohlstand für alle*, p. 163.
3. Erhard, *ibid*, pp. 7–8.
4. Erhard, *ibid*, pp. 150–158.
5. *Report on the competitive capacity of the European Community*, Professor Uri and others, Office for Official Publications of the European Communities, Luxembourg, 1973.
6. There is no equivalent in English for this term (meaning literally 'hand-work'), which covers some 125 occupations requiring a high level of skill including engineers, builders, vehicle mechanics, electricians, radio and TV repairs, plumbers, butchers, bakers, hairdressers and opticians.
7. For example, see *Bericht der Bundesregierung über Lage und Entwicklung der kleinen und mittleren Unternehem*, Deutscher Bundestag, 7 Wahlperiode, Drucksache 7/5248.
8. See *The defence and promotion of the self-employed and small business in the Federal Republic*, Paul Schuiker.

CHAPTER 7

The small firm in the French economy

Pierre-Yves Barreyre

Introduction

France emerges today as an industrialised country where small independent firms account for a substantial part of the gross domestic product and play an important role in the geographical and political balance of the country, as well as in the adaptability of the economy to new challenges in the national and international environment.

Petites et Moyennes Entreprises (PME) are the object of a great deal of attention at the moment, even though their proprietors tend to be suspicious of government help. The state's recent interest in these organisations on a 'human scale' is probably not simply a question of fashion. Whatever the immediate reasons, it reflects a turning point in social history; there is a general recognition that large organisations and urban industrial concentration are not a panacea that will bring about prosperity and a high quality of life.

At a time when the development of our society seems to have seized up with problems – unemployment, the energy crisis and so on – the potential importance of small firms in the renewal of industry and economic flexibility is thrown into relief. The creation of new firms and the rise of small-scale industry are now official objectives in the new industrial strategy and a number of recent measures have been taken with these ends in mind.

It would be unfortunate if, in this new mood, we should succumb to hasty generalisation and fall into the romantic trap of wishing to preserve the past. If the results of the new measures to help small firms have so far been disappointing, it is perhaps partly because those involved have had too distant and either too generalised or too partial a view of their subject. In fact, PME are a heterogeneous group which includes both some which are remarkably innovative and forward looking, and others where management is very backward. It is essential to recognise this. There are, of course, some problems common to all PME, but they do not necessarily dominate in all the thousands of firms, some of which may be large in relation to their market while others play a marginal role. Some face competition only from other small firms, some are in direct competition with large firms.

Social and economic change and their consequences for PME

To understand the position of PME today, it is helpful to review the changes that have affected them over the last quarter of a century. At the outset it is necessary to remember that France is a country in which geography favours agriculture and in which the population density is still less than 100 persons to the square kilometre.

Leaving aside the exceptional concentration in Paris, the majority of the population live in small towns and villages. This has favoured small units in preserves, dairy products, farming, forestry and wood-working industries, as well as rural activities catering for local consumption.

Because of its advanced political, scientific and cultural development (national unity was realised in the 17th century), France was one of the first countries, after Britain, to industrialise.

The value system of the French has been strongly marked by the influence of the Roman Catholic church and by the logic of written law. There is a certain mistrust of profits made out of the creation of large financial or commercial empires and a propensity in business affairs to go for stability and order, rather than adventure. The French temperament, which we think is individualistic and imaginative, naturally favours 'do-it-yourself' and accommodates itself well to small business.

The trades unions are generally hostile to the capitalist system and this has encouraged industrialists to hive off activities in small units where union influence is less felt. (See P. Y. Barreyre, *L'impartition, politique pour une entreprise competitive*, Hachette, Paris, 1968, chapter 2. The concept of *impartition* illustrates the modern approach to production sharing – sub-contracting, etc. This policy of transfer to external partners counteracts the propensity to vertical integration.)

From 1884 to 1954 France was strongly protectionist and self-sufficient and, except towards its colonies abroad, had only a weak propensity to export; small firms, therefore, were well suited to the needs of a relatively restricted market. Also, in the period of post-war reconstruction, business conditions were very favourable and there was a blossoming of new firms.

Between 1954 and 1974 the French economy underwent a major transformation marked by the following developments:

- The opening of its markets to foreign competition (the Common Market, GATT, etc.);
- dismantling of its former colonial empire;
- population growth and urban concentration;
- expansion and modernisation of the industrial structure;
- an industrial policy which favoured industrial concentration, particularly between 1967 and 1975;
- rapid modernisation of distribution (central purchasing, exceptional growth of supermarkets);
- inward investment by foreign companies (particularly from the United States);
- development of modern management techniques.

For small firms these changes had the following consequences:

1. The disappearance of numerous firms in outmoded activities:
   - small agricultural holdings;
   - small, non-specialised shops (grocers, ironmongers, general food stores, etc.);
   - some traditional crafts.

2. The elimination of many enterprises in sectors which were in rapid decline (leather industries), finding it difficult to remain competitive (textiles and clothing), or in which the technology now required large amounts of capital (food processing, paper, cement, etc.).

3. The maintenance and development of small firms in sectors favoured by economic growth and led by large firms:
   - firms in construction;
   - firms acting as suppliers or sub-contractors to large firms (engineering, metal working, plastics, miscellaneous components);
   - firms providing business services (transport, data processing, consultancy, security, repairs and maintenance).

4. The breakthrough of appreciable numbers of small firms in certain growth markets: leisure industries (winter sports, camping, travel); pharmaceutical laboratories; toys; electric household appliances; electronics and instruments; mechanical handling and contractors' equipment; new forms of distribution, etc. Some of these enterprises have grown into large organisations; for example, BIC, Carrefour, Club Méditérannée, Moulinex, Matra, Pochain, Rossignol.

In fact, the average size of business establishments has increased and the share of small independent firms in national output has fallen significantly. This decline is not fully reflected in the official statistics, which include as independent enterprises some firms which are, in fact, subsidiaries of large firms.

Despite their relative decline, PME have adapted well to economic change and remain important, their total number having remained fairly stable during the period. The decline of the share of small firms in output should not be interpreted as a failure to respond to the challenge of events. In numerous cases success has carried PME into the upper size group, also many large firms have grown primarily through the absorption of smaller ones.

It is difficult to assess the position of PME since 1980, since the necessary statistics are not yet available. There has been a substantial increase in company failures and in mergers. The failures have been largely concentrated among small enterprises; large firms in difficulty have received state support for social reasons, while small businesses feel unprotected by the government, which imposes on them increasing taxes and social costs and constraints. Since the 1981 elections the new socialist government has done its best to keep in touch with PME employers, but these are the ones usually suspicious of the socialist programme; they want lower social costs and taxes, rather than more state support.

The economic crisis which is common to the whole western world has particularly affected the number of small-scale industries: certain capital goods, parts and components, construction and some industries subject to strong competition from countries with lower labour costs, for example. Some small firms have collapsed with cash-flow problems, a few resulting from excessive delays in the settlement of accounts with larger customers in both the private and public sectors, at a time when bank credit has been severely restricted. Some of these firms were basically sound, innovative and with good prospects.

Defining and classifying PME

For administrative and statistical purposes, PME are normally taken as enterprises employing less than 500 persons, though this limit is lowered to 200 or even 100 in certain sectors, such as textiles or services. Sometimes a turnover figure is used, sometimes equity capital. 'Small' (as distinct from medium) firms in manufacturing are generally regarded as those employing less than 50 persons. This is also the level above which social legislation requires enterprises to have works' councils for employees. Particular legislative provisions apply to craft enterprises belonging to professional bodies and, finally, firms with a turnover of less than Fr. 500,000 are exempt from the need to register for value added tax.

In 1980 there were 3.6 million PME enterprises in France. However, it is reiterated that the statistics available in France are not comprehensive. The total of 3.6 million enterprises breaks down as follows:

1. 200 very large firms (more than 5000 employees)
2. 2,500 large firms (more than 500 employees)
3. 30,000 medium firms (between 50 and 500 employees)
4. 130,000 small firms (between 10 and 50 employees)
5. 500,000 family firms (with just one worker plus family assistance)
6. 3,000,000 self-employed (individuals with professional or craft skills)

The problems of small firms

If we exclude those firms which have obviously not achieved the absolute minimum efficient scale for their field of activity, PME have a number of important strengths: in particular, a simple form of organisation which allows flexibility and speed of decision; and where the owner manager has the necessary qualities, they are excellent vehicles for innovation.

Against this, PME are vulnerable when they are in a situation characterised by one or more of the following:

- capital intensive technology with low capital-turnover;
- rapidly changing technology in an expanding market which requires heavy investment expenditure;
- uncertainty in products and markets. A large firm can be diversified, but a small firm is likely to be heavily dependent upon a narrow range of activities;
- excessive dependence upon a small number of customers, as in sub-contracting in the electronics and watch industries;
- management continuity which depends upon health or age of the proprietor or his family situation.

A further problem in France, as elsewhere, is lack of capital, often referred to as the 'Macmillan Gap'. For some investment, medium-term finance may be available from specialised institutions, such as the Crédit d'Equipement PME (CEPME), which results from a merger between two big financial organisations. It is controlled by the French state. These institutions, with the banks, provide mortgage finance for the purchase of certain assets or loans of other kinds where security is available, perhaps from a credit guarantee association. The small firm, however, finds it difficult to obtain risk capital without loss of independence. The few initiatives taken to resolve this problem have not been very fruitful and PME criticise the bureaucratic attitudes of the banking system, the greater part of which is nationalised in France.

It is also evident that PME find it difficult to diversify – into foreign markets, for example. In many cases PME do not have the resources to make the necessary investment in export markets before they can be made profitable, nor can they offer a sufficiently attractive range or volume of business available to their foreign customers. From this has come the idea of small firm consortia to increase the bargaining power of members with customers, suppliers and banks.

A statute of 4 February, 1959, allowed the formation of the *société conventionée*, which is a subsidiary of several firms, none employing more than 500, created to carry out certain functions on behalf of its members (eg common purchasing). The *société conventionnée* from a legal point of view is just like any private company with limited liability, but its capital is not fixed. The advantage for its members is that the capital they subscribe can be written off against their profits for tax purposes. In theory this arrangement is very attractive, but in practice the administrative complications have discouraged its use and the provisions are now rarely used. Since 1967, inter-firm collaboration has received a new stimulus from the introduction of GIE (Groupements d'Intérêt Economique). GIE, which are not restricted to PME, allow their members to act in common without losing their independence and have the legal power to borrow and engage in commercial activities, but have no capital. All profits or losses flow through to members so that the GIE have fiscal transparency and are not subject to taxation. GIE are mainly used for joint marketing activities and, in all, some 3,000 have been formed.

Another major problem for small firms is the weight of government legislation affecting taxation, social and economic matters. Not only does the owner manager have difficulty in finding his way through the labyrinth of regulations, but he must devote a large part of his time to mastering their complications and filling in the numerous forms he receives when he should be building up his business. As M. Gauban, a former President of the National Union of PME has written, parodying Kafka: 'The torture chains of small firms are made of ministry red-tape'.

Social legislation being particularly developed in France, the owner managers complain not only of the restrictions it results in and the cost, but also of the distressing degree of government surveillance and inspection that follows from it. Recently, several chief executives have been taken to court following accidents in their establishments.

In a few cases prison sentences have resulted and this, together with the more frequent irritations arising from visits by factory inspectors and tax officials, have been taken as an attack on private enterprises. Businessmen feel that they are unloved and vilified by the bureaucracy, by universities and so on. If they succeed it is exploitation, if they fail it is mismanagement; they feel, in short – and in this they are partly right – that their role in society is not understood. In addition, agricultural enterprises received much better treatment from the state than industry. PME do not actually want special treatment, but they do want the government to do its job in improving the services for which it is responsible, a more prosperous economic environment and some relief from the shackles which restrict small firm managers.

State assistance

There are, in fact, a whole range of measures to support, promote and help small firms and also to favour the new enterprise. Until recently, however, there has been no coherent policy but rather a series of isolated and unconnected initiatives. These include:

–   tax reliefs with the object of stimulating new enterprise formation, decentralisation to the depressed areas, investment, collaboration amongst PME, etc;
–   special loans for firms in difficulty, exporters, innovation, etc;
–   subsidies or grants for decentralisation, job creation for young workers and the development of new technology, etc;
–   low rate credit by Agence Nationale pour la Valorisation de la Recherche (ANVAR) for innovation;
–   measures in favour of sub-contracting and access to government contracts;
–   the setting up of institutions to provide equity capital for PME; for example, the Sociétés de Développement Régional (SDR), the Institut de Développement Industriel (IDI) and the Société de Financement de l'Innovation (SFI);
–   training and information exercises for small-firm managers to promote exports among other objectives, such as the PME pilot operations carried out in the regions;
–   efforts to stimulate exports by small enterprises;
–   reliefs from certain social security payments to encourage recruitment by small firms, etc;
–   advisory services: the creation of a team of about 200 industrial management advisors working from local Chambers of Commerce and Industry.

Some of these measures were aimed at allaying the fears of small firms about foreign competition – the measures to aid collaboration amongst small firms are a case in point. Others stem from the idea that PME are an essential element in regional development. Some result from the initiatives of prominent politicians wishing to act on a specific problem or simply to satisfy part of the electorate. Some were inspired by foreign example; the work of the Small Business Administration in the United States has in particular been influential. Finally, many of these measures were dictated by unfavourable conditions in particular sectors of the economy.

In general, the measures taken have been too sparing, too timid and insufficiently known amongst the firms that they affected. They have also sometimes been too complicated in application for small firms with limited management resources.

In the last few years, following the appointment of an Administrative Director for PME at the Ministry of Industry, Commerce and Crafts, a major effort has been made to co-ordinate action, to disseminate information about the measures taken and to adapt them more closely to the needs of small business. It has also been recognised that the economy of a country like France needs the entrepreneurial spirit and that this should be encouraged, not only by institutional changes, but by a change in the whole cultural background in which small business operates.

Statistical sources and references

P. Y. Barreyre, *L'Horizon économique des Petites et Moyennes Entreprises* (Unpublished doctoral thesis, Grenoble University, 1967).

P. Y. Barreyre, *Stratégie d'innovation dans les Moyennes et Petites Industries* (Editions Hommes et Techniques, Paris 1975).

R. Brocard et J. M. Gandois: *Grandes Entreprises et PME* (Economie et Statistiques (INSEE) no 96, January 1978).

Caisse Nationale des Marches de l'Etat: *Les PME dans l'économie francaise après la récession de 1974-1975* (Bulletin CNME ler trim, 1980).

Credit d'Equipement des PME: *Les Petites et Moyennes Industries en 1981* (Survey, SOFRES, June 1981).

INSEE (Institut National de la Statistique), Annuaire Statistique de la France 1980 – Nombre d'entreprises au ler janvier 1980.

CHAPTER 8

Small business in Italy - the submerged economy

Julia Bamford

The contrasts and paradoxes of the Italian economy are a constant source of amazement for observers in other industrialised countries. The Italian economy is permanently in a state of crisis, so much so that for Italians the very word has been stripped of all real meaning. New expressions have to be invented to cope with problems such as an inflation rate of over 20%, a devalued currency, high unemployment, wildcat strikes and mastodontic state corporations staggering under mountains of debt.

Nonetheless, amid this apparently hopeless situation, Italy has managed in recent years to consolidate its position as the West's sixth economic power and both in 1979 and 1980 achieved the fastest growth rate of any of the EEC countries. This is all the more remarkable in a country short of agricultural land and almost bereft of raw materials.

Italy defies most attempts at generalisation. It is a country of contrasts: both an advanced, developed country and an under-developed one, both western European, integrated into the Common Market, and Mediterranean. Few visitors can fail to be struck by its visible prosperity, at least in the northern and central regions. Whereas sales of new cars in other European countries declined sharply during 1981, in Italy they increased by 3.7%. Italy also leads the rest of Europe in the number of people owning second (holiday) homes.

The Italian economy has very advanced and profitable sectors which use a technology second to none (Olivetti, Pirelli); its know-how is exported the world over (SNAM Projetti). It boasts the largest automated car plant in Europe (Fiat) yet its large state industries are deeply in debt and notorious for their bureaucratic, inefficient management (mostly due to appointments made for political reasons), poor production statistics and even worse labour relations.

The most interesting, lively and profitable sector of the Italian economy is, however, the small business sector. This ranges from medium-sized privately-owned firms down to cottage industries. It is in these small businesses that the famous Italian initiative, imagination and entrepreneurial spirit have full play. Many of these enterprises are based on another fundamental Italian institution – the family – and it has been argued that they have done much to maintain the prosperity of the Italian economy over recent years. This part of the economy has also been described as the *economia sommersa* (submerged economy) so called because it manages to avoid many of the government's laws and regulations regarding taxes, social security, wage rates and regulations of working conditions. The term covers a broad collection of micro firms whose performance is difficult to assess statistically for precisely the same reason that many of them exist, that is by avoiding a large part of government regulation and assessment.

The importance of small business to the Italian economy as a whole has no equivalent in other western developed countries. Statistics which deal with this sector of the economy will for many reasons tend grossly to underestimate the real phenomenon – much of the really submerged sector will not be included. Even so the following table[1] clearly shows the numerical importance of small businesses within the Italian economy.

Table 1

Percentage employed according to size of firm in the manufacturing industries of some OECD countries

	Number of Employees			
	1-9	10-99	100-999	over 1000
Italy (1971)	23.2	31.2	29.8	15.7
France (1962)	19.2	27.0	36.5	17.3
Belgium (1963)	7.4	26.7	41.1	24.8
West Germany (1961)	13.2	22.6	36.0	28.2
United States (1963)	3.3	22.9	43.3	30.5
United Kingdom (1968)	18.9		46.1	35.0

The smallest category (1-9 employees) is very significant with respect to all the other countres.

According to census data, in Italy during the twenty-year period from 1951 to 1971, the number of people employed in manufacturing industries was consistently above half the total number employed. However, when evaluating this data we must take into account that many of those employed in small firms escape being counted in official statistics altogether because their contribution to the production process is made up of *lavoro nero* (black labour). There have been various attempts at estimating the extent of this phenomenon. Numerous observers agree that 'black labour' involves at least 1,500,000 people in Italy – the equivalent of one-tenth of the working population. According to one survey of the female population of four small towns in the provinces of Bologna and Modena in 1972, 1,060 workers were using their own homes as their workplace compared to the 311 which the offical census registered.[2] In the textile and clothing industry the 1971 official census figures show a total of 896,000 persons employed. At the same time a study of 32 provinces unearthed at least another 500,000 'black' workers in the submerged part of this sector alone.[3] Sometimes, however, these same unofficial workers are registered as agricultural workers in census data, since they work in both sectors at the same time. This is also true of some types of public employees whose working day often ends at 2.00 p.m., leaving them free to participate in the submerged economy for the rest of the day. A survey of the Marches region which tries to estimate the real extent of 'black labour' shows that 27.5% of the employed population is involved.[4]

Why does Italy have so many small firms compared to other imdustrialised countries? What are the functions fulfilled by small business in the Italian economy? It may be supposed that small businesses fulfil the same functions in Italy as in other industrialised economies – experimenting with new models, they operate in those areas which are technologically backward, and in productive processes which larger firms no longer find it profitable to undertake in rapidly changing market conditions; and they have a complementary function with regard to the large firm. This is certainly the case in Italy but it is only a partial explanation of why small business is of such notable relevance to the economy as a whole.

Economists have suggested as an explanation the existence of a dualistic development of the economy with a technologically advanced sector on the one hand and a more under-developed sector on the other. The modernisation of the economy has slowed down or even stopped, thus accounting for the large number of non-rationalised productive systems left over. This would explain in terms of 'backwardness' the presence of so many small firms fulfilling rearguard functions in out-of-date uneconomic productive processes.

Suzanne Berger sees the survival of economically backward small firms as a consequence of the peculiarly Italian way of dealing with those problems connected with cyclical fluctuations of the economy.[5] The small business sector in this explanation becomes the fundamental stabilising element of the system. The labour force is expanded or contracted according to the needs of the market. In times of expansion more workers are absorbed into the more modern technologically advanced sector (largely industry), but when recession arrives the excess manpower is re-absorbed into the more backward sector (small firm). Thus the small firm constitutes a reserve of manpower for the large firm.

This model is even more effective if applied to the agricultural sector; workers leave the industrial sector in times of recession to go back to their former agricultural activities (usually on their own smallholding). This is true not only of workers in large industrial firms but more often of those employed in medium-sized and small firms. In most areas of the Marches region we find the family at the centre of this osmosis between agricultural and industrial occupations. Some of the structures which exist in this region are very complex and economically can be put to many uses. A common case is that of the family in which grandparents and parents work on their smallholding while sons and daughters are employed in one of the manufacturing processes undertaken by small local firms. Another case is that in which the whole family is employed in manufacturing whilst in their free time they work their smallholding. The flexibility of both cases is evident: in a slack period agriculture provides a means of making a living to the whole extended family.

It is certainly true that explanations of the prevalence of small firms in the Italian economy emphasising their residual character with respect to the more technologically advanced sectors can effectively be verified in some cases. However, this view has serious limitations, mainly because it explains only the backward, static, inefficient, aspects of the system. Many small firms cannot be fitted into this category. Their steady growth over the last ten years, the fact that a large percentage of their products are exported, together with the relatively high level of technology used in some production processes, show that in fact a large number of small firms are dynamic, efficient and rationalised. A demonstration of this is that many large firms have in recent years begun a process of decentralisation of production involving many small firms. In the Bergamo area quite advanced technological types of production are carried out in small workshops, surrounding the parent factory. Although Fiat's factory in Turin, Mirafiori, is the largest in Europe, its latest factories in the south of Italy are all relatively small.

The small firm is, to a much greater extent than the large firm, influenced by the international division of labour. The Italian economy is very much conditioned by being a latecomer to the industrial development of western Europe. Development is seen as the ability to export. Italy's economy is characterised by high numbers of exported goods requiring a low level of technology in their production (leather goods, footwear, textiles, wood, steel), and a relatively low level of exported goods requiring high innovative levels of technology (aeroplanes, chemicals, precision instruments, electronic machinery). In the last few years there has been an increase in exports of those goods requiring an intermediate level of technology (inorganic chemicals, petroleum derivatives, automobiles, buses and commercial vehicles, machinery). Amongst the thirteen most industrialised countries Italy accounts for 7% of exports of goods with intermediate levels of technology and 8% of goods with low levels of technology.[6] It we break this 8% down we find that for some types of production the percentage is considerably higher: for example in the shoe sector Italian exports amount to 54%, furniture 17% and clothing 24%.

We see clearly here the importance of the less advanced sectors of the economy in relation to exports. It is easily demonstrable that it is in just these sectors that many small and micro firms have contributed to the growth of the last ten years. In the shoe industry the five largest firms account for only 9% of the total, 2.4% of fixed investments and 4.3% of employees. The furniture industry's five largest firms account for 9.4% of total production, 10% of fixed investments and 6.6% of all its employees. The statistics for other sectors with 'mature' technology mirror this tendency almost perfectly.

Table 2

The distribution of employees in sectors with traditional technology by numbers of employees (1971).[7]

	Up to 9 %	10-99 %	100-499 %	500 and over %
Textiles	15.20	35.03	32.29	17.48
Clothing	34.77	30.84	23.53	10.85
Shoes	29.95	46.07	20.71	2.64
Leather and pelts	29.12	51.14	17.08	1.94
Wood	58.05	32.66	8.18	0.96
Furniture and furnishings	37.13	49.03	11.85	1.72
Non-ferrous minerals	17.61	46.59	26.57	9.23
All manufacturing industry	23.34	31.16	22.24	23.25

Traditional production processes are often dispersed in small units and these find in their size their economic *raison d'être*. 'Mature' technology linked with reserves of labour and low labour costs, unstable demand and scarce control of markets, are a further encouragement to the small firm. But this type of industry is very much bound by two important restrictions: quick changes in fashion and consumption which are the cause of fluctuating demand, and the nature of the technology employed which is not susceptible to labour-saving innovations. In other words, the greater part of Italian industry has to produce goods which are highly labour intensive with an extremely variable demand and unchanging technology. Under these circumstances it is hardly surprising that the small firm brings high degrees of flexibility to the system through the adaptability of the small entrepreneur, the use of the family as a productive unit, the putting out system and 'black' labour in general. The hosiery industry, for example, has an average of 10 employees in Italy, 100 in France and Germany and 110 in the USA, and the figures clearly demonstrate a difference in the approach of these countries to industrial organisation.

The analysis of the Italian economy as a dualistic system, large industry and small industry, advanced and mature technology, an official and an unofficial economy, has been inspired by the analysis of the American industrial system made by Averitt.[9] Averitt describes the industrial system of America as consisting of a central part with high capital intensity, large corporations, technologically advanced sectors, control over all productive processes and advanced marketing techniques. The other side of the coin is the peripheral part of the American economy which consists of small or medium sized firms, traditional types of production, high labour intensity, interstitial production and highly specialised markets. The important difference between the Italian economy and that of the USA is that, proportionately, in the Italian economy the peripheral part assumes a fundamental importance, as we have seen in Table 1, whereas in the USA the large corporation overshadows the rest of the economy.

Italy has in recent years experienced a phenomenon which begins to blur the distinctions of dualism. Large firms have started to decentralise several phases of their production process, subcontracting substantial parts of it to satellite firms. We are beginning to witness a large scale restructuring of industry at a national level. Observers tend to attribute this phenomenon to a reaction by large firms to the trade union activities of 1968–70 with their consequent legal and contractual concessions. It has been the large firm which has been called upon to pay the high cost of these concessions. Decentralisation of production can be seen as an answer on the part of the Italian industrial system to the sharp rise in labour costs and the general upheaval and disruption of work caused by both official and unofficial strikes.[10]

The relatively high labour costs and high levels of labour unrest depend (especially the former) on the particularly large share of employers' contributions to social security funds in total labour costs. The total bill for 'dependent' labour in 1970 was made up of 72% gross pay and 28% social security payments, compared with averages for Common Market countries of 81% and 19% (West Germany's bill was 87% and 13%). The high labour costs have done much to weaken the financial position of firms in a recession – and particularly in conditions of slack demand but still rising costs – because social security contributions rise alongside wages paid. While in theory high labour costs apply to both small and large firms, the large firm cannot escape government vigilance and avoid paying its dues. The small firm declares less and therefore pays less tax, VAT and social security contributions. While social security payments are much higher for firms in Italy than in other European countries, the number of self-employed persons in Italy is also higher (40% of the total working population). In practice this means that large firms and dependent workers pay the bulk of the national social security bill leaving the small firm and self-employed worker to reap the eventual benefits while paying less than their share.

Trade union relations and the general well-being of the dependent worker are regulated in Italy by the *Statuto dei Lavoratori.* This was the main concession resulting from the long series of strikes and political turmoil of 1968-70. The workers, especially those employed in large firms, emerged from this period with greater protection and substantial gains. Wages were indexed to cost of living increases on a sliding scale; there was no longer a link between productivity and wages; wage differences between different types of workers were abolished; working hours were reduced; workers were entitled to some study leave during the year at full pay and finally working conditions were much improved.

The *Statuto dei Lavoratori* fixes at 15 the number of employees in a firm below which Article 35 is no longer applicable. Article 35 establishes extremely rigid and difficult conditions for the sacking of an employee, making it difficult to get rid of any worker. It also establishes compulsory membership of a trade union. Thus, we can see how the firm with less than 15 employees has much more flexible labour relations and can, in times of slack demand, get rid of excess labour. Labour relations in general in small firms are easier because the entrepreneur establishes a personal relationship with his employees, invoking their loyalty, making them feel involved personally in the progress of the firm.

Although the small firm is becoming increasingly important throughout the whole of Italy, there are certain regions in which it is particularly prevalent. These regions are in the centre and north-east of the country, the Marches, Emilia Romagna, Tuscany and the Veneto.[11] Those employed in firms with less than 290 employees are 86% of the employed population in the Marches, 81% in Emilia Romagna, 79% in Tuscany and 75% in the Veneto. The increase over the last 20 years has been considerable and has been accelerated since the 1971 census. From 1961 to 1971 the increase in firms with under

250 employees was 12.4% in the Marches, with the other regions following close behind.

What is the particular socio-economic structure of these regions and what have they in common which enables the small firm to bloom and flourish here? Production in these regions tends to be organised in very specialised areas; for example, almost all the firms in the Prato area are involved in the textile industry; Carpi in Emilia Romagna and its surroundings specialises in knitwear; Modena and Reggio Emilia have important agglomerations of engineering firms. Often the reasons why one industry is attached to one town or district are cultural or historical in origin. Today's growth is linked to long artisan traditions or share-cropping agriculture. Artisans and peasants are capable of dealing with machinery and varied technologies, have developed sound business sense and entrepreneurial spirit, while at the same time maintaining their local value systems. Recent economic developments have interesting historical precedents. Complex cultural elements are implicit in the process. Culture here does not mean just attitudes and ways of thinking but the whole complex of reciprocally accepted ways of behaviour, mutual expectations and customs.

One of the characteristics which these regions held in common was their agricultural organisation, based on the share-cropping system (*Mezzadria*). It was common in other parts of Italy but in these regions it lasted longer, in some cases until after the last war. It can easily be demonstrated that the origins of the entrepreneurial spirit, propensity to hard work, a high degree of flexibility and a remarkable technical capacity are to be found in the share-cropping families of these regions. At the same time, in the small towns spread throughout the area, a thriving artisan class with strong traditions of craftsmanship catered for the needs of the landowners, who stimulated a demand for all manner of goods and services.

Carpi is a good example of the continuity shown in the economic development of a town. Its historic manufacturing traditions and organisation are surprisingly similar to present-day ones. The system of production was based, from the 16th century onwards, on the merchant/entrepreneur figure who employed cottage labour, collecting the finished products (straw hats and straw coverings for wine bottles), which he then sold in the markets and fairs in the surrounding districts. Today the product has changed (fashion knitwear), the market has become international, but the entrepreneur still fulfils the same function and most of the work is done on a putting out basis.

The historian Braudel has demonstrated how the evolution of Europe has depended on the birth and growth of 'everyday' structures, on the capacity of individuals, their creativity and inventiveness, on merchants and their ability to react to the various changes in their society. Nowhere is this to be seen more clearly than in Prato. Much of its thriving textile industry depends on structures and traditions which have been operating in Prato almost uninterrupted for centuries. The high degree of technical ability, professional skills and entrepreneurial spirit available permit the town to export in the face of competition from the newly industrialising countries. A large part of the organisation of production is done on a putting out basis, one entrepreneur organising the various phases of production and the marketing of the finished product. This system can only work within tight time schedules and with reciprocal faith, both in the ability of the outside worker to produce high quality goods at the agreed time and on the entrepreneur's ability to provide a constant stream of work and keep his designs and raw materials abreast of fashion. In Prato, textiles are sometimes carded, spun, woven and dyed with each operation completed in a different micro factory. Only the packing and shipping is carried by the entrepreneur.

Prato is looked upon with surprise and suspicion for the miracle it works daily. Many observers find it hard to understand how Prato expands and consolidates a productive sector which is generally considered too 'mature' for advanced industrialised countries. Prato manages to make innovations and to change and adapt continuously the range of products it produces, keeping constantly in touch with the demands of the market as regards price, taste and quality. Its mode of production is flexible, often its phases are fragmented between firms, and productive units (13,000 firms with 63,000 employees) compete with each other. The organisation of the Prato model of production is based upon a diffused entrepreneurial spirit making use of highly qualified professional workers. 40% of employees work in firms with less than 10 employees and only 28% in firms with more than 50 employees. The great majority of those employed in an artisan workshop belong to the same nuclear family.

Prato, as an industrial area, is characterised by its specialisation in one productive sector, in the growth of external economies which this specialisation induces. It manages to maintain high rates of production by keeping dependent workers to a minimum and offering them a form of participation in the firm's success. Increases in productivity bring about increased profits and, consequently, higher wages. Ironically, this has happened in a town with a Communist municipal government, whilst nationally the Communist Party has been agitating for the abolition of production bonuses in the factory.

The 'Censis' survey of Prato reports that among the population interviewed, the highest values were ascribed to 'hard work' (62%), followed by 'spirit of initiative and enterprise' (52%). Working hours were found to be 15% longer than the national average. Most of those interviewed who were engaged in some form of working activity linked to the textile industry had a working day of 11 hours or longer. Incomes were also found to be higher than the national average, although the interviewers suspected gross under-estimation on the part of interviewees, judging from their large, expensive houses, cars and consumer durables. In fact, the number of cars per 100 inhabitants is 31% higher than the national average.

Paci has suggested that the family plays a crucial role in the industrial development of modern Italy, thus highlighting another of its distinguishing features.[13] The extended family, with relations cohabiting in the same household, has always been more common in Italy than in northern Europe. The role of the family is illustrated in the Marches region, which has been remarkably successful in resisting the recent recession.

Like the other central and north-eastern regions, the Marches also tends to have towns given over to one specific type of industrial activity. In the valleys of the rivers Esino and Misa, the knitwear industry is widely dispersed in a myriad of micro factories and workshops. In the last 20 years the industry has gone through a profound crisis and a consequent decentralisation of productive activity. Much of the labour force is female, the male population being occupied in agriculture. The small firm tends to be dependent on larger firms for the marketing of its final product, much of which is exported; thus, the vagaries of fashion and international demand are felt keenly. Small firms tend to be of two types: one consists of businesses attached to larger firms in northern Italy, which prefer to have their products manufactured in small firms with lower labour costs and fewer union problems. The other type of firm exists because it succeeds in continually changing the final product to keep up with oscillations in fashion. Some completely autonomous firms manage to produce finished goods and market them independently. These firms usually farm work out to small workshops or female workers working at home and paid by the piece.

The shoe and footwear industry is concentrated in the provinces of Ascoli Piceno and Macerata. It has three characterising features: the low number of workers in each unit, the high level of artisans working in the sector and the increasing incidence of exports upon total production. In these districts the growth in numbers of artisan workshops is tied to the diffusion of work on commission. Both constant demand, which has been sustained for several years, and an effective sales network, which is indispensable in an industry like this where exports are paramount, have led many artisans and ex-workers to set up on their own account. Many larger firms have sub-contracted some of the processes of shoe-making to small workshops. The difference between small and medium-sized firms or artisan workshops is almost non-existent, since the most relevant differences depend on the quantity produced. Therefore, in this sector, there are no technological limits to the decentralisation of production. There are, however, barriers produced by the market; in other words, small firms depend on having goods commissioned by larger firms or by import-export concerns. In some periods, increases in demand are passed on to artisan workshops, which may make the whole article or some part of it.

This is a picture of two typical small industries in the Marches. How has family structure and the share-cropping type of agricultural organisation influenced the extraordinary growth which this region has witnessed in the last 20 years? The head of the peasant family has, for generations, been used to organising the working life of his whole extended family, which at times numbered 40 heads. Thus, within the family itself, a division of labour was created. Historians have recorded for generations the laboriousness of the Marches family and travellers marvelled at the resistance to fatigue and the speed at which the women of the household worked.

Towards the 1950s, the share-cropper began to buy the piece of land which he had worked. To do this, he had to enter into debt; thus, partly by choice and partly by necessity, peasants began to work in the small industries which were beginning to set foot in the region. Increasingly one or more of the peasant family began to work in the small factories and artisan workshops or, in the case of the women, to take in work at home. The realisation of the economic benefits accruing from a combination of part-time farming and industrial employment accentuated even further the already existing division of labour in the family. The final step, which only a limited number of families ever arrive at, is that of the micro entrepreneur. The ex-share-cropper gradually develops into worker and part-time farmer, then artisan and, finally, becomes a small businessman. In the transition period, much of the industrial work is performed by various members of the family and later, in the small firm stage, by more distant members of the kinship group. The base of this activity remains the land; it is the kingpin upon which the entire system revolves and is of prime importance as a source of capital accumulation and labour, and it is used to help keep costs to a minimum.

The research Brusco undertook in Bergamo investigates two observations – that metallurgical firms were increasingly commissioning work outside the factory and that those workers in small firms who produced goods commissioned in this way enjoyed worse working conditions, lower wages and overtime pay than their fellows in large firms. The research tries to demonstrate whether, in fact, the level of technology used in the small firm was more backward than that of the large firm or, if it was, as some observers have suggested, of an even higher technological level than that of the large firm.[14]

The analysis carried out by Brusco confirms that within the complex set of operations necessary for the production of a particular article, there are a series of interstices within which economies of scale are of secondary importance. Some of the small firms in the survey operated within these interstices, whilst others produced finished goods and were small only apparently; in reality, they co-ordinated the work of a much greater number of workers than those on their official payroll.

Many factories decentralise the whole of the production apart from the construction of prototypes and the final assembly. This is the case, for example, of factories with less than 30 employees which produce scales, dishwashers or machinery for the paper industry and textile machinery.

As far as the types of machinery involved in the production of various goods are concerned, half the firms in the survey, even those with less than 10 employees, attained a level of technological sophistication equivalent to semi-automatic machinery. The rest of the firms surveyed used techniques based on manually controlled machinery. Some processes, it must be remembered, cannot use automatic or semi-automatic machinery, whether they take place in large or small factories.

It can be seen that in Bergamo technological requirements are less a determinant of the size of the firm than has usually been supposed. Technology imposes a minimum size on working units; for example, in the moulding of refrigerator bodies. This does not mean, however, that many working units of this type have all to work under the same roof. Each working unit can exist by itself in a whole network of small workshops and factories, each producing the same product, or part of a finished product.

According to Brusco, the factors which favour the agglomeration of working units together in one large factory are fundamentally organisational, whereas those leading in the opposite direction are political. Entrepreneurs find it easier to control workers in several small factories rather than in one large one, even though, from an organisational point of view, the latter might be more efficient. As long as the control of the workforce is feasible, optimum technology only determines the scale of the working unit and the entrepreneur decides how many working units to group together in one factory. Only when the entrepreneur prefers to disperse the working units do the limits imposed on the optimum dimensions of the working units become operative.

The importance of the small business to the Italian economy is the result of many factors – technological, political, social, cultural and historical. All of these combine to give the sector its present-day dynamism and force. Although, as we have seen, some sectors depend on 'mature' technology (shoes, furniture, clothing), they also depend on good design and ability to change quickly to meet the demands of fashion. It is, above all, these latter qualities which qualify the Italian small business and help it to survive, notwithstanding mounting competition from newly industrialising countries. Another new and important facet of the small business in Italy is the decentralisation of production operated by large firms. Although the decision to decentralise was initially political, it also makes sound economic sense because even the large firms can in this way avoid paying at least some part of its crippling labour costs.

The development of the small business economy which we have seen principally in the central and north-eastern regions of the country is rapidly extending to other areas, both in the north and the south. Unlike many other European small businesses, the Italian small firm is not a large firm in embryo but is born and destined to remain small. It is left very much to its own devices and receives precious little in the way of government help and assistance. Unfortunately, because of its size, the small firm cannot undertake research into possible technological innovations and it is here that its main weakness lies. Suitable government assistance and co-ordination in this field would do much to ensure the survival and development of small businesses in Italy.

References

1. Table adapted by Bagnasco A., *Tre Italie – la problematica territoriale dello sviluppo italiano* (Mulino, Bologna, 1977).
2. See Bergonzini, L., 'Casalinghe o lavoranti a domicilio' in *Inchiesta* 1973.
3. Frey L., 'Le piccole e medie imprese industriali di fronte al mercato del lavoro in Italia', in *Inchiesta*, 1974.
4. Bugarini, F., 'Il lavoro irregolare e l'attività per l'auto consumo', in M. Paci, *Famiglia e Mercato del lavoro in un Economia Periferica* (Franco Angeli, Milan, 1980).
5. Berger, S., 'Uso politico e sopravvivenza dei ceti in declino', in *Il caso italiano*, ed. Cavazza, F. L., and Granbard, S. R. (Milan, 1974).
6. Statistics from Bagnasco, *op cit.*
7. ISTAT.
8. See Sylos Labini P., *Saggio sulle classi sociali* (Bari Laterza, 1974).
9. Averitt, R. T., *The Dual Economy* (Notton & Co., New York, 1968).
10. See Podbielski, G., *Italy's Development and Crisis in the Post-War Economy* (Clarendon Press, Oxford, 1974).
11. Regional distribution of the small firm has been discussed at length – see Bagnasco, *op. cit.*
12. See *Il caso Prato*, ricerca a dura del CENSIS ETAS libri (Milan, 1980).
13. *Famiglia e Mercato del lavoro in un Economia Periferica*, ed. Paci, M. (Franco Angeli, 1980).
14. Brusco, S., 'Economie di scala e livello technologico nelle piccole imprese', in *Crisi e Ristrutturazione nell' Economia Italiana*, ed. Graziani, A. (Einaudi, Turin, 1975).

NOTE: This chapter is an abridged version of a contribution to *Non-Conforming Radicals of Europe: The Future of Industrial Society*, edited by Edward Goodman and published by Duckworth, 1983. Both books have their origins in the Acton Society conferences at Siena.

CHAPTER 9

Public policy and small firms in Britain

M. E. Beesley and P. E. B. Wilson

I Introduction

The appointment of the Bolton Committee in 1969 to investigate the problems of small firms and to make recommendations signalled the beginnings of an overt small business policy by the British government. The publication of its report in November 1971 promoted an unprecedented interest in the small business sector, partly through its examination of hypotheses about the disadvantages widely thought to be suffered by small firms and partly through its recommendations for remedial action by government.[1] Many of the government measures covered by this article then began to emerge; and the genesis of public policy towards small business gained momentum.

The growth of concern about small business is shown by statements made by government spokesmen. Diagram 1 measures parliamentary interest in terms of entries to Hansard from 1964, when small business first began to be debated seriously. It shows the beginnings of parliamentary interest in the mid-1960s, the perceptible impact of the Bolton Report of 1971 and the subsequent rapid increase in the number of debates, questions and answers in Parliament, all reflecting a deepening interest in the contribution of small firms to economic growth and employment creation and a concern with the impact of government policies on the health of the sector.

Before the Bolton Report assistance to small business was *ad hoc*, emerging as a by-product of policies towards industrial efficiency, training, technology, organisation and location. The prevailing philosophy at the time of the Bolton Report was one of bigness, exemplified by an industrial policy of rationalisation and re-organisation into larger units capable of exploiting supposed economies of scale. For instance, the Industrial Reorganisation Corporation (IRC), established in 1966, was charged with the reorganisation and development of firms in strategic industries in order to ensure that Britain competed effectively in world markets, where large size was considered a necessary minimum condition for survival and growth. According to Allen, the IRC embodied the development of more systematic government intervention in industrial activity.[2] Although the origins of this new approach are related to the promotion of large-scale enterprise, in them also lies the simultaneous development of government policy towards small business.

This chapter describes how government policy towards small business has evolved since the late 1940s and particularly since the Bolton Committee published its findings in 1971. Government assistance measures until August 1981 are listed in Appendix A.

II Definitions

The problem of definition of a small business is usually resolved by referring to the Bolton Committee, which concluded that a 'small firm' is recognised by three broad qualitative characteristics. First, a small firm tends to have a relatively small share of its relevant market, implying that it has little or no power to affect either price, quantity or its environment. It is possible, however, for a small firm to have a large share of a small, yet specialised, market niche. Second, a small firm has no formalised management structure; rather, the owner manager is responsible for decision-making. The extent of formalisation will vary among firms, however, since as the firm grows, personal owner management is replaced partially or wholly by professional management. Third, a small firm is independent of the control of a parent company, implying a certain freedom to make decisions. But even if management is free from interference by a parent company, it is usually inextricably dependent on its network of advisers, customers, suppliers and bankers; so these attributes are not necessary conditions for being deemed small business, although most commentators assume they are.

In practice, only close observation will reveal whether the small business exhibits these characteristics. In fact, the behaviour and role of the owner manager or entrepreneur are the key to a working definition. In small firms, the behaviour of the owner manager and the behaviour of the firms are synonymous. But in order to determine changes in the small firm population over time, numerical definitions are also necessary. These are given in Appendix B. Generally, small firms in manufacturing are defined as those with fewer than 200 employees, and in other sectors a variety of definitions applies. A further breakdown is given in Appendix C.

III Government policy towards small business

In seeking to establish whether successive British governments have developed explicit policies towards small business and what the nature of these policies is, we look to three main indicators of public policy. These are:

a) specific small business legislation;
b) statements made by government spokesmen; and
c) other general legislation and measures to assist small business.

Britain has no specific small business legislation, such as is to be found in other countries, particularly the United States. For instance, the Small Business Act of 1953, which established the Small Business Administration, was the culmination of a long history of legislation sympathetic to the independent business, starting with the Sherman Anti-trust Act of 1890.[3]

Without the benefit of such obvious small business legislation, evidence must be sought elsewhere. The Bolton Committee, established by a Labour government sympathetic to the needs of small business, is an appropriate starting point. When the committee published its report of 1971, the Conservative government welcomed its findings and recommendations and the Secretary of State for Trade and Industry at the time commented that he was well aware of the place of small firms in the economy and that he would ensure that 'their interests be taken into account in the formulation of policies.'[4] In June, 1972, the Under-Secretary of State with responsibility for small firms, a new office recommended by the Bolton Committee, stated that he was 'determined that small firms should be allowed to flourish and thrive in the freest possible environment, unhampered by unnecessary restrictions and unintentional discrimination'.[5]

The Conservative government acted on many of the report's recommendations, although it was firmly against discriminatory policies in favour of small firms. It intended, rather, to remove past discrimination and to prevent discrimination being built into new policies, by considering measures necessary for the encouragement of individual enterprise and initiative.[6]

These intentions were largely in sympathy with the Bolton Committee's conclusions that positive discrimination by government in favour of the small business was unjustified and that the sector could perform its self-regenerative function unaided. It did find that government had imposed a number of unintentional disabilities on the small business which amounted to discrimination.[7] We discern a commitment to these sentiments by the Conservative government, with policies oriented to two objectives: first, providing an environment in which the small firm could thrive, free from interference of any kind; and second, removing the discriminatory impact of existing legislation. Although evidence of the former is not presented here and, indeed, would be hard to gather, there is evidence of the removal of discrimination and the exemption of small firms from certain statutory obligations which, it was alleged, bore more heavily on them than on larger firms.

The Labour government of 1974 adopted the same objectives. The accent was to be on the avoidance and elimination of unintentional discrimination against small firms and the creation of a climate favourable to their growth, including protection from the alleged anti-competitive market practices of the giant companies.[8] In June, 1974, the Minister of State for the Department of Industry pointed to the Labour government's 'unambiguous' commitment to an active small business sector, which was 'important in regional terms as a seedbed of regional growth and a source of diversification and balance in the industrial structure'.[9]

The Labour government's attitude to small firms soon acquired a flavour of more direct support. The Secretary of State for Industry in 1975 signalled a 'more vigorous' policy for small firms because of their local markets, their labour intensiveness and the close relationship between the owner manager and the workforce. Indeed, he claimed to be 'strongly sympathetic' to small firms and 'strongly in favour' of their development.[10]

This theme was further developed with the appointment, in September 1977 of Lord Lever, a senior minister in the Labour government, and Robert Cryer, the Under-Secretary of State in the Department of Industry with responsibility for small firms, to make a special study of their problems and to recommend and initiate remedial action.[11] Increased official concern for small business was clear and implied that existing policies were not adequate. As a result of Lord Lever's study, budgetary measures were announced in October, 1977, and April, 1978, as 'part of a developing policy in which Government was going to show a continuous responsiveness to the needs of small firms'.[12]

In January 1977 the government appointed the Wilson Committee to inquire into the role of the financial institutions and the provision of funds for industry and trade, and the committee's study of the financing of small firms was published in March 1979.[13] Some of the recommendations of the Committee were subsequently accepted, particularly those involving no apparent change in government policy. Of the recommendations which could be classified as discriminating in favour of small business, the proposals for small firm investment companies, an English development agency and a publicly underwritten loan guarantee scheme were the most extreme, signalling the government's willingness to depart even further from its adherence to a non-discriminatory small business policy. In the event, the loan guarantee scheme and certain investment incentives were introduced, though in a more muted form than that proposed by the committee; but no agency has yet been sanctioned.

The Conservative government of 1979 pursued the trend towards greater intervention in the affairs of small business started by the previous Labour government. David Mitchell, Under-Secretary of State responsible for small firms, stated in July, 1980:

'There is a recognition on both sides of the House of the importance of small businesses as the seedcorn from which wealth creation and many jobs in the future will come. We have far too few such businesses. We need many more. The balance between the incentives to start a business, the hurdles which face those who start and the burdens they have to carry has been tipped so far that a logical person has not felt it worthwhile to start a business. The government are engaged in a threefold task. The first is to identify the burdens and to pull them down, to identify the hurdles and take them away, so that it is easier for people to start. Secondly, we have to increase incentives for them to do so. Thirdly, we have to look at the problems of financing those who have started, or are seeking to start, in terms of the money inside the business as well as incentive in terms of what one can take out in reward for success'.[14]

We recognise in this statement the familiar references to the removal of discrimination. But for the first time a government spokesman also spoke of a need to encourage the birth of small firms (as opposed to their survival and growth) and to do so directly. Not only were incentives mentioned as an element of policy, but the allusion to the problems of financing new and small firms presaged further direct preferential assistance by government. Although the Bolton Committee had expressed concern about the low birthrate of new firms, successive governments had introduced few measures specifically oriented to new firms. Nevertheless, there has been a consistent increase in the numbers of new businesses since 1974 and a clear upward trend in these numbers since the mid-1960s, illustrated in Diagram 2. Policy has changed simultaneously with this increase.

In spite of this revealed change of direction over the last few years, government spokesmen still did not espouse a policy of direct preferential assistance. For instance, in March 1981 the Under-Secretary of State for small firms reiterated the government's policy of removing obstacles and burdens and changing the overall climate in which the small business operated.[15] There was no allusion to direct preferential assistance. Yet the Business Opportunities Programme was launched by the government in May 1981 following the measures introduced in the 1981 Finance Act, another example of direct encouragement of small business. The programme's emphasis on raising national awareness of the opportunities and rewards of small business adds a new dimension to government policy: in order to stimulate the birth of more new ventures, the government is pursuing an aggressive marketing campaign throughout the country. This programme is described in more detail below, as are the other measures which constitute a *de facto* preferential policy.

In July 1981 the Chief Secretary to the Treasury outlined four elements of industrial policy, namely the reduction of inflation, 'supply side' policies to improve market efficiency, privatisation and market-orientation of the public sector and support for industry in selected areas. It was intended to stimulate the economy by removing constraints to the efficient operation of market forces and by improving incentives to enterprise and rewards for effort, including the introduction of measures to stimulate the growth of small business.[16]

IV   Government aid

This section is confined to general comments about the nature and extent of government assistance; individual measures are detailed in the appendices. With the exclusion of assistance that has either a marginal or no effective bearing on small firms at all, it is possible to identify three groups of measures and, within these, a number of sub-groups.

These three groups also mark the three periods of government activity noted below. The first, from 1946 to 1960, covers the period when there was no specific assistance to small business. The second period, up to 1970, was characterised by government measures to remove discrimination. The third period covers the measures introduced since the publication of the Bolton Report, including most instances of positive discrimination. This period can be further sub-divided into two five-year periods, and a perceptible increase in the number of direct measures is recorded in the latter period. Each type of activity, with varying incidence, has been continuous, once commenced.

Indirect assistance
The first group consists of those measures that indirectly or inadvertently have a significant effect on small business, despite their

intended universal application. These are listed in Appendix A (*A*). They can be further grouped into regional or locational assistance, such as the Scottish and Welsh Development Agencies which have their own small business units; assistance with production efficiency, training and advice, such as the Industrial Training Boards; technological assistance, as with the National Research Development Corporation; and assistance consistent with economic policy, as with industry aid under the Industry Act of 1972. Until 1976 there was no marked trend in indirect assistance, although in the last five years there has been a perceptible increase over the earlier period which, as illustrated in the appendices, has been characteristic of all government assistance to small business.

Most indirect assistance falls into the regional assistance sub-group and the bulk of this has been introduced since 1970. A substantial amount of indirect assistance has been directed to small firms (Appendix A, A5) and local authorities have also begun to orientate their employment policies increasingly towards small business (Appendix A, A6), which effectively gives small business policy a greater regional and local dimension.[17] Indeed, pressures brought to bear by local government organisations on central government to devolve additional small business powers down to the local level are increasing; many local authorities are considering directly investing in small businesses through local enterprise trusts set up for this purpose.[18]

The introduction of training and advisory assistance, although directed at industry as a whole, can have a considerable impact on small business. This has been recognised by successive governments, culminating in a more direct approach in recent years. The recognition that small firms are at a particular disadvantage in the market for training and advice is based on the limitations of the owner manager with regard to personnel training expertise. Although such expertise is available externally in appropriate amounts, for most very small firms it would still be uneconomical to employ it. Despite the availability of industrial training and advice from the public sector at subsidised rates, small firms have not been successfully absorbed into training schemes.

The removal of discrimination
The second group has been imposed to remove discrimination against small firms, largely by exempting them from various statutory obligations. These are listed in Appendix A (*B*). It is based on the proposition that management resources in the owner managed small firm are lumpy: they consist essentially of one person. To add to them involves a disproportionately large increment, not easily

achieved. The small firm, on this view, is placed at a considerable disadvantage relative to larger firms, with respect to any given commitment requiring managerial attention. Large companies need only make relatively small adjustments in resources to deal with the duties and obligations imposed on industry and commerce by the government.

Within this group are three distinct sub-groups. Regional exemptions cover industrial and commercial construction allowances to small firms; administrative exemptions, such as disclosure exemptions under the Companies Act and the revision of statistical surveys of small firms; and exemption under economic and social policy, particularly the recognition that the smallest firms should not be subject to dismissal procedures under the Employment Act.

Direct preferential assistance
The third group of measures discriminates specifically or positively in favour of small business by providing resources and inducements. The majority of measures falls into this category, most being introduced after 1971 with a clear upward trend in the last five years. As Appendix A (*C*) illustrates, direct assistance since the Conservative government came to power in 1979 has accelerated further, despite the claim that such positive discrimination was never to be incorporated into government policy.

It is possible to distinguish three broad types of assistance within this group. The first type is designed to further the general aims of economic and social policy and consists of measures to promote exports, particularly among small first-time exporters, rural development, regional assistance and technological change. The second type is designed to favour small firms *per se* and consists of non-financial aid such as training and advisory services, and the Small Firms Division of the Department of Trade and Industry is charged with overall responsibility for the sector. The third type consists of financial measures, such as fiscal incentives to establish new ventures, increasing the rewards due to entrepreneurial activity, improving the supply of venture capital to new firms and providing a loan guarantee scheme for loans made by the private sector banks. We observe two main features relating to these financial measures. The first is the marked increase in direct financial measures relative to other direct measures over the last few years; and the second, the focus on new ventures relative to established small firms.

V   Summary
The large number of measures described in the appendices confirms that since 1946 there has been continuing government interest in

small business, but until the 1960s, assistance tended to be *ad hoc*, incidental and indirect. Thereafter, increasing official concern with small business was reflected in the introduction of direct preferential treatment – more than 75% of government measures are either direct or related to the removal of discrimination. Over two-thirds of all measures have been introduced since 1970 and over one-third since 1975. The trend to greater direct assistance is likely to continue unabated. In the period 1946–70, 53% of all measures introduced were direct, while in the period 1971–81 this proportion was 64%, rising to 72% in the five-year period up to 1981. (A notable feature is the orientation of assistance towards manufacturing, which reflects the concern with the declining position of manufacturing in the economy; only one-third of the assistance has been directed to non-manufacturing enterprise.)

Certain other developments may be mentioned as being significant for the future. Support for the introduction of advanced technology in small firms is increasing, either through indirect assistance or financial aid and incentives. Co-operative enterprises may have a brighter future; the government is backing the Co-operative Development Agency. The attention of central and local government has, in the last few years, been increasingly drawn to businesses owned by immigrant minority groups.[19]

The continued shift of regional investment incentives and other aid away from large to small firms is the likely consequence of the continued structural decline of some of Britain's older industries. And the emphasis on the employment creation impact of small, rather than large, firms will tend to strengthen the flow of assistance to the former in the assisted areas and in nominated inner city areas.[20] The introduction of Enterprise Zones in the 1980 Finance Act provides another channel for more direct assistance and local authorities have shown greater interest in increasing the flow of resources to small business.

Central and local government, the nationalised industries and quasi-government bodies provide a large resource for exploitation by small firms in the form of procurement contracts. The Bolton Committee noted that certain government departments were unintentionally favouring large firms when placing procurement contracts, and recommended that purchasing policies be investigated with a view to increasing the flow of products and services provided by small firms to the government.[21] Consideration might be given to the system adopted in the United States, whereby a minimum proportion of these contracts is guaranteed for small firms. Meanwhile, the present government has improved the flow of information about procurement contracts through the Small Firms

Information Centres.

Further developments in policy may result from a coincidence of arguments in favour of small-scale organisation, growing in popular appeal, and the specific need of large firms to shed labour in response to economic recession, to make profit centres more responsive to the business and social environment and to accentuate entrepreneurial initiative. The activities of such nationalised industries as the British Steel Corporation in assisting small firms are only one step removed from hiving off certain production tasks into sub-contract work, where executives and/or skilled workers might take severance or redundancy pay and start up a new enterprise supplying their former employers, the necessary administrative, managerial and other assistance being provided by the parent company. Large private companies could, it is argued, be persuaded to act in a similar fashion where there were clear economic and social benefits, or where redundancies were inevitable.

Finally, it may be asked if the diversity and complexity of the provisions for assistance described in this chapter are reaching a point where consolidating legislation for small firms is indicated.

Diagram 1:
Index of Parliamentary interest in small business, 1964-1980

Number of entries in Hansard, consisting of debates and written and oral questions and answers

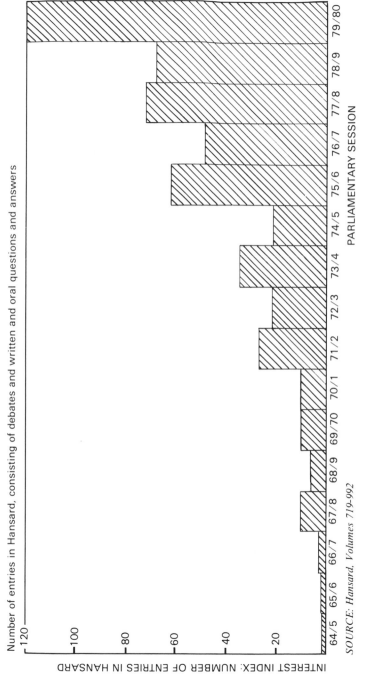

INTEREST INDEX: NUMBER OF ENTRIES IN HANSARD

PARLIAMENTARY SESSION

SOURCE: Hansard, Volumes 719-992

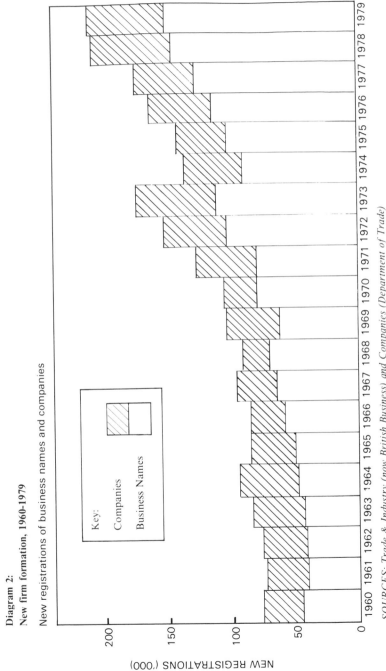

Diagram 2:
New firm formation, 1960-1979

New registrations of business names and companies

Key:

Companies

Business Names

NEW REGISTRATIONS ('000)

200

150

100

50

0

1960 1961 1962 1963 1964 1965 1966 1967 1968 1969 1970 1971 1972 1973 1974 1975 1976 1977 1978 1979

SOURCES: Trade & Industry (now British Business) and Companies (Department of Trade)

Appendix A

Summary: Government assistance 1946-1981

A. Indirect assistance
1946 – 1960
A 1   National Research Development Corporation (1948, manufacturing) (1)
A 2   British Productivity Council (1952, manufacturing)
1961 – 1970
A 3   Industrial Training Boards (1964)
A 4   Highlands and Islands Development Board (1965, retailing and services excluded)
1971 – 1981
A 5   Industry Assistance (1972, manufacturing)
A 6   Local Authority Assistance (1972, mainly manufacturing)
A 7   Scottish Development Agency (1975)
A 8   Welsh Development Agency (1976)
A 9   Development Board for Rural Wales (1976)
A10   National Enterprise Board (1978, manufacturing)
A11   European Investment Bank (1978, manufacturing)

B. The removal of discrimination
1961 – 1970
B 1   Industrial Development Certificates (1962)
B 2   Office Development Permits (1965)
B 3   Companies Act Disclosure (1967)
1971 – 1981
B 4   Employment Legislation (1971)
B 5   Value Added Tax (1972)
B 6   Price Code (1973)
B 7   Collection of Statistics (1973)
B 8   Competition Policy (1980)

C. Direct preferential assistance
I.   Economic & Social Policy
1961 – 1970
C 1   Small Exporters Policy (1961, manufacturing)
C 2   Low Cost Automation Centres (1961, manufacturing)
C 3   Council for Small Industries in Rural Areas (1968, manufacturing, services and tourism)
C 4   Export Award (1969, manufacturing)
1971 – 1981
C 5   Crafts Advisory Committee (1971, manufacturing)
C 6   Export Educational Visits (1974)
C 7   Co-operatives & Common Ownerships (1976)
C 8   Small Firms Employment Subsidy (1977, manufacturing)
C 9   Computer Aided Production Management (1977, manufacturing)

C10 Market Entry Guarantee Scheme (1978, manufacturing)
C11 Business Opportunities Programme (1981)

II. Non-financial direct assistance
1961 – 1970
C12 Industrial Liaison Service (1961, manufacturing)
C13 Production Engineering Advisory Service (1967, manufacturing)
C14 Consultancy Scheme (1968, manufacturing)

1971 – 1981
C15 Small Firms Division (1971)
C16 Small Firms Information Centres (1973)
C17 Small Firms Counselling Service (1976)
C18 Collaborative Arrangements (1976)
C19 Management Education (1976)
C20 Manufacturing Advisory Service (1977)
C21 Small Factory Units (1977)

III. Financial direct assistance
C23 Corporation Tax (1972)
C24 Close Companies (1972)
C25 Rating Relief (1974, retailing and services)
C26 Capital Transfer Tax (1975)
C27 National Health Service Dispensing (1978, retailing)
C28 Income Tax (1978)
C29 Loan Guarantee Scheme (1981)

Summary of assistance: number of measures per period
1946 – 1960: 2
1961 – 1965: 8
1966 – 1970: 5
1971 – 1975: 15
1976 – 1981: 18

Note: Year refers to year of inception; manufacturing refers to industry coverage; where no industry is mentioned, the assistance applies to all, or most, industries.

Appendix B
Statistical definitions of small business

Industry	Definition (upper limits)
Manufacturing	200 employees
Retailing	£185,000 p.a. turnover
Wholesale trade	£730,000 p.a. turnover
Construction	25 employees
Mining and quarrying	25 employees
Motor trade	£365,000 p.a. turnover

Miscellaneous services	£185,000 p.a. turnover
Road transport	5 vehicles
Catering	All except multiples and brewery managed public houses

Note: Limits have been revised upwards since the Bolton Commission originally published these definitions. Figures are at 1978 prices. (Interim Report of the Committee to Review the Functioning of Financial institutions, *op. cit.* p. 43).

Appendix C
Specific definitions relating to Government assistance

Type of assistance	Definition (upper limits)
1. Definitions relating to employment	
EIB loans	500 employees
Proprietory company (proposed)	50 employees
Employment Act exemptions	20 employees
CoSIRA aid	20 employees (skilled)
Export award	200 employees
Export visits	200 employees
Employment subsidy	200 employees
Computer Aided Production Management	500 employees
Industrial Liaison Service	500 employees
Consultancy Scheme	500 employees (min. 25)
Collaborative Arrangements	200 employees (manufacturing)
Manufacturing Advisory Service	1000 employees (min. 100)
2. Definitions relating to annual turnover	
Companies Act disclosure exemption	£1 million
Proprietory company (proposed)	£1.3 million
VAT registration	£15,000
Price Code exemptions	£1 million (manufacturing)
	£250,000 (distribution, services)
	£100,000 (professions)
Competition Act exemptions	£5 million
3. Miscellaneous definitions	
EIB loans	£20 million (fixed assets)
IDC exemption	50,000 square feet
ODP exemption	30,000 square feet
Proprietory company (proposed)	£650,000 (bal. sheet total)
Small Exporter Policy	£100,000 (export value)
Corporation Tax reduced rate	£80,000 (profits)

References

1. *Report of the Committee of Inquiry on Small Firms*, Cmnd 4811, (HMSO, 1971)
2. Allen, G. C., *The structure of industry in Britain*, (Longman, 1970), p. 162.
3. For example, see Bruchey, Stuart W. (ed.), *Small business in American life* (Columbia UP, 1980).
4. John Davies, *Hansard*, 3 November, 1971, column 188, vol. 825.
5. Anthony Grant, *Hansard*, 12 June, 1972, column 1061, vol. 838.
6. *Trade & Industry*, 13 July, 1972, vol. 8, no. 2.
7. *Bolton Report*, pp. 87–91.
8. John Fraser, Minister of State for Prices & Consumer Protection, *Trade & Industry*, 28 October, 1977, vol. 29, no. 4.
9. Eric Heffer, *Trade & Industry*, 27 June, 1974, vol. 15, no. 13.
10. Tony Benn, *Trade & Industry*, 28 February, 1975, vol. 18, no. 9.
11. *Trade & Industry*, 10 November, 1978, vol. 33, no. 6.
12. Harold Lever, *Trade & Industry*, 21 April, 1978, vol. 31, no. 3.
13. *The financing of small firms*, Interim report of the committee to review the functioning of financial institutions, Cmnd. 7503, HMSO, 1979.
14. *Hansard*, 30 July, 1980, column 1553, vol. 989.
15. John McGregor, *British Business* (was *Trade & Industry*), 13 March, 1981, vol. 4, no. 11.
16. Leon Brittan, *British Business*, 24 July, 1981, vol. 5, no. 13.
17. Greater detail is contained in Wilson, P., *Local authority assistance to small business* (Conference paper, UK Small Business Management Teachers Association, Manchester, September, 1980).
18. Windas, S. (ed.), *Local Initiatives in Great Britain* (Foundation for Alternatives, 1981).
19. See, for example, House of Commons, Home Affairs Committee, *Racial Disadvantage: West Indians in Business in Britain* (HMSO, 1980).
20. Storey, D. J., 'Small firms and the regional problem', *The Banker*, November, 1980, vol. 130, no. 657.
21. *Bolton Report*, p. 80. Public sector buying power amounted to £22,000 million in 1980 (*The Times*, 12 January, 1981).

CHAPTER 10

Small business research in Britain

James Curran and John Stanworth

Introduction

The vast increase in interest in the small enterprise in Britain since the early 1970s among politicians, civil servants, the mass media and the general public has been accompanied by an equally substantial increase in related research activities. Yet the findings of this research have failed to make much impact. Politicians and others continue repeating the same myths about small businesses or, at best, misrepresent the findings of one or two research projects; for example, on the job-generation potential of new small businesses. But, overall, it is the sheer lack of awareness and understanding of this research which stands out.

It might be said, also, that even among those engaged in promoting small enterprise activities, awareness of the full range of recent research is still somewhat patchy. Partly, this is a matter of available time: keeping up with research disseminated through an exceptionally wide range of outlets is not easy. But partly, also, there is the echo here of the familiar meaningless division in Britain between those who 'do' and those who 'theorise'. Essentially this is a false division, yet it tends to produce inward looking attitudes among those who would classify themselves into either grouping, cutting them off from the experiences and insights of the other group.

The original stimulus for the present survey was the tenth anniversary of the publication of the Report of the Committee of Inquiry on Small Firms – better known as the Bolton Report. The influence of the report on thinking about the small firm in Britain would be difficult to overstate. It aroused enormous interest among policy makers and its findings have formed the bedrock of virtually all research since 1971. It is also, therefore, an obvious starting point for any review of small business research in Britain.

Prior to 1971, the literature on the small firm was relatively small and overwhelmingly American in origin. Classic studies, such as those of Collins et al. (1964), Mayer and Goldstein (1961), and McClelland's (1964) theoretical contribution are obvious examples here. The absence of any larger literature or specifically British research was not serious, since interest in the small enterprise in Britain was very limited. Big was seen as beautiful and growth was seen as the key to the treasures of increased economies of scale. Management and business education largely followed this fashionable consensus. The Bolton Report coincided with the backlash against that consensus. Faced with a dearth of research on the small firm in Britain, the committee commissioned several studies which subsequently resulted in 18 research reports (Bolton Report, 1971, Appendix 3). These reports can be seen as the beginnings of modern research in the area though, in fact, some of the most influential studies in the field were being conducted concurrently and independently (Ingham, 1970; Boswell, 1973; Stanworth and Curran, 1973; Batstone, 1975, for example). By more recent standards, many of the Bolton research reports may seem superficial, both theoretically and methodologically, but they helped to establish the notion that policy making and prescription for the small business required a firm under-pinning of research-based knowledge.

Small firms: definitions and statistics

Two basic questions discussed at length in the Bolton Report were the conceptualisation of the small firm as a socio-economic entity and the size of the small firm population in Britain. Conceptualisations are, by their nature, matters for continuous debate, because they are unavoidably and logically required for theorising of any kind, yet there are always arbitrary judgements about what constitutes the relevant domain of interest. No amount of evidence can do more than inform such judgements. On the other hand, such conceptual problems cannot simply be brushed aside. Defining what is meant by the small firm is not only a prerequisite for research itself, but is also required for realistic policy-making by national and local government. Moreover, it is apparent, even to the casual observer, that there is no easy solution to the problems of deciding what constitutes a small enterprise, if only because of the sheer variety of small-scale economic endeavour in Britain.

The Bolton Committee initially defines the small enterprise in terms of a qualitative, trichotomous notion stressing small market share, personalised management and independence of decision-making (Bolton Report, 1-2). The Committee immediately ran up against probl. ~ns of converting their notion into quantitative indicators suitable for empirical research. Their solution – the adoption of non-comparable numerical definitions for each of the nine sectors of economic activity covered by the inquiry – has had considerable influence on thinking and research since 1971.

But for the main sector with which the Committee was concerned – manufacturing – it is now widely recognised that the upper size limit adopted of 200 employees was probably too high. Research being conducted at the same time as the Committee's deliberations generally adopted an upper limit of 100 employees (Batstone, 1969: 10; Ingham, 1970: 65) and some researchers who adopted a similar definition to the Committee have since expressed doubts on their decisions (for example, Curran and Stanworth, 1979b: 428).

Whether similar doubts should be expressed about the definitions for the other eight sectors is less certain, since there has been relatively little subsequent research, but certainly inflation has meant problems for the monetary definitions adopted for the motor trades, wholesale trades and miscellaneous sectors.

Employing its set of nine quantitative indicators, the Report concluded that there were around 820,000 small firms employing 4.4 million, or about 30% of the labour force, in the sectors covered (Bolton Report, 1971: 33–34). But, as the Report also pointed out, the Committee had omitted a very substantial amount of other small business activity, accounting for around a further 430,000 enterprises employing 1.6 million people so that, overall, approximately a quarter of the national labour force worked in small enterprises (Bannock, 1976: 14–15).

The sectors excluded from consideration by the Committee included agricultural enterprises and many kinds of financial and personal services. For example, most estate agents, insurance brokers, accountants, general practitioners, dentists and lawyers are in small partnerships. Leaving aside agriculture, the neglect of these other areas could be argued to constitute a rather backward-looking view of industrial society. The essential character of advanced industrial societies is that they are shifting their major economic emphasis from manufacturing to various kinds of tertiary activities (Galbraith, 1969; Bell, 1974; Gershuny, 1978), and we might have expected the Committee to be much more actively interested in the small firm in the economy of the future.

It has to be said at once that the numerical picture of the significance of the small enterprise in Britain in 1983 appears no clearer than in 1971. Indeed, in some respects it is becoming less clear. Small businessmen have always been reluctant to provide even elementary statistical data for the Census of Production and other official information-gathering exercises. National government is the only body with the resources and the authority to collect such information but politicians have become increasingly unwilling to burden small businessmen with additional paperwork and, more recently, the wish to reduce public expenditure has led to the reduction of information collecting on the small enterprise. The Wilson Committee, reporting in March 1979, selected only three sectors in which to estimate the number of small enterprises and the changes since 1971. In manufacturing it found that between 1963 and 1973 (then the most recently available data) there had been an increase in the number of small firms from 66,000 to 74,000. As Table 1 shows, more recent data from the Census of Production indicates that there were almost 87,400 small manufacturing enterprises in 1980. Between 1963 and 1973 the proportion of the total manufacturing labour force employed in small firms marginally fell from 21.3% to 20.7%. For 1980, Census of Production data, based on establishments, suggests a figure of 24.3%. These figures have to be treated with great caution because of the difficulties involved in gathering statistics in this area, including changes in the basis of collection, but the conclusion drawn by the Wilson Committee – which seems borne out by more recent data – was that the number of small manufacturing firms has increased since 1971, with their share of the labour force and output also increasing slightly.

The other two economic sectors discussed by the Wilson Committee were retailing and construction. They concluded that small firms in the retail sector had continued to decline and the decline showed signs of accelerating towards the mid-1970s (Wilson Report: 48–49). However, as Kirby (1982) has pointed out, there is no reason to assume this decline will continue. There may well be a minimum number of small shops which will successfully survive in a modern economy because they fill a genuine economic role. In construction, the statistics were again far from satisfactory – for example, an additional 25,000 firms were identified and added to the list in 1973 and further changes in data collecting were expected to lead to the discovery of more small firms in this sector (Wilson, 1979: 50), but the proportion of small to large firms had, apparently, stayed broadly constant during the 1970s period for which data was available.

A broad picture of the small firm in three sectors of the economy is insufficient to arrive at any generalisation about either its relative importance or expected changes in its position. The lack of accurate data is a profound disadvantage for researchers, but it is even more serious for policy makers. Successive governments have developed policies for encouraging small firms and argued that they have a central role to play in the redevelopment of Britain's economy yet, at the same time, the statistical base required for rational policy making is being dismantled or allowed to wither away.

Other forms of small enterprise

On the whole, most observers take a conventional view of the small business, concentrating on manufacturing and distribution enterprises of the traditional variety. But in the 1970s we became more aware of other varieties of small enterprise, whose contribution to the economy is gradually being recognised as having considerable significance. Two examples are franchising and the so-called 'black economy'.

A fairly rapid expansion of franchising in Britain has occurred since 1971, though important areas of the economy have long been dominated by the franchise pattern of distribution, most notably brewing and car and petroleum distribution. Essentially, franchising consists of an organisation (the franchisor) with a market-tested product or service, establishing contractual relationships with franchisees (typically, aspiring small businessmen), who set up their own business to operate under the franchisor's trade name and market the product or service in the manner specified.

Franchisors are generally larger firms (though by no means always), and franchisees are generally small businessmen. The central characteristic of the franchised business is the special relationship between companies, where the central aim of one of the companies is to promote a large number of smaller, satellite enterprises. The main advantages to the franchisor are the rapid achievement of national coverage for his product or service, with most of the capital put up by others (the franchisees) and the elimination of many of the motivational and personnel problems which increasingly arise where face-to-face customer contact occurs at a large number of outlets remote from head office.

Given that our economy is moving towards a greater emphasis on tertiary activities, it is also moving towards being a service economy highly suited to franchising. The service sector more frequently has a pattern of dispersed outlets directly serving local markets, with the crucial customer contact occurring through these outlets. It is not surprising, therefore, that franchising in Britain appears to have undergone a substantial expansion in the 1970s, although exact figures are hard to come by (once again, no official statistics are available, or collected, on this form of economic activity).

Franchise World, the industry's trade magazine, lists nearly 100 franchises currently on offer in Britain, ranging from the long-established Wimpy fast food operation with over 400 outlets in Britain alone, to examples of the more recent trend of major companies converting some of their operations to a franchised form. Among the latter are Booker McConnell and the British School of Motoring.

The British Franchise Association, to which most of the major franchisors in Britain belong, claimed that its members had over 4,000 outlets in operation by the end of 1982 and that expansion was occurring at around 10% a year. Most of these outlets have been set up since the early 1970s. To this figure might be added the 35,000 tenanted public houses (Brewers' Society, 1982), since the tenant-brewer relationship is often seen as closely resembling a franchise relationship and the Brewers' Society themselves refer to these outlets as 'independent small businesses operated by tenants'. Further, there are around 24,000 retail petrol outlets of which over half are franchised to independent owners (Institute of Petroleum, 1983), plus around 7,600 franchised car dealerships (Motor Agents' Association, 1983). Finally, it is also possible to add around 25,000 voluntary group wholesale-retail franchises (Kirby, 1983), such as Spar, Mace, VG, and similar operations in other areas of retailing, for instance, photography.

It is impossible to put an exact figure on the number of franchised enterprises in Britain, but the total may be as high as 80,000. A not insignificant number of these have come into existence in the last decade and they represent a net addition to the number of small enterprises in Britain. What is more, we expect this trend to continue both in the form of new operations and existing businesses converting to the franchise form. In other words, official statistics might suggest a continued decline in the conventional small business over time, but to take this as a firm indication of a decline in the small business in Britain generally is to ignore these recent developments in the economy.

This latter point is further underlined when we shift attention to the black economy, taking this to refer to the production of goods and services for gain, which is systematically concealed from official notice in order to avoid the payment of tax or other dues to the State. Estimates of the extent of the black economy vary, but a recent analysis argued that it might be worth around 15% of the national income, equivalent to unpaid taxes of around £11.1 billion a year (Feige and McGee, 1982), although the Inland Revenue's estimate is about half this – a still significant figure.

Undoubtedly, the major factor in the development of the black economy was the introduction of VAT in 1973, which taxed a whole range of hitherto untaxed services and activities and promoted wholesale evasion. Other factors which have been suggested as playing a part include increases in National Insurance contributions, employee protection legislation and technological change (Gershuny and Pahl, 1980). For instance, in several kinds of activity, such as building maintenance and decoration, new tools and methods have made it easier for the unskilled to offer their services (for cash) and consumers have shifted their allegiance from previous conventional suppliers to these new sources. A large proportion of the black economy is, in fact, small business activity. Some will consist of legitimate small businesses becoming illegitimate and some will be the seeds of tomorrow's legitimate small businesses; having expanded within the black economy, they become big enough (and visible enough) to register and trade officially, but many of these small enterprises will remain outside official knowledge forever. Again, the argument can be made that the trend towards the black economy is now an established aspect of our economy and represents another important outlet for entrepreneurial talent.

A third, if less important, form of small enterprise is also worth mentioning in estimating the significance of the small business in Britain's economy. According to Chaplin (1982) there were over 500 producer co-operatives in being at the beginning of the 1980s, about 15 times the number at the beginning of the 1970s. Most are very small measured in terms of the numbers involved (over 80% have fewer than 19 workers), but, because most are so recently established, there is potential for further growth. And, says Chaplin (1982: 94), co-operative enterprises appear to survive at least as well as conventional companies. Again, therefore, an unconventional form of small enterprise appears to be expanding.

Few would want to enter a serious dispute on the exact number of small firms in Britain, or whether this number is increasing or decreasing – the data are simply too imprecise. The official data suggest only a moderate decline in the 1970s, but against this we have to note a number of counter-trends. The fashionable vogue for bigness, so prevalent in the 1960s, has long been reversed. Economists who stressed economies of scale in the past now balance this with an equal emphasis of the *dis*-economies involved. Concentration in many sectors is not increasing rapidly (Lawson, 1982) and much new technology, from plastics to microprocessors, is highly suited to small-scale production. Overall, therefore, we would argue that the small enterprise sector is remarkably healthy in the 1980s, despite the onset of the severest recession since the 1930s.

The owner manager and the entrepreneur

The characterisation of the small businessman offered in the Bolton Report was uni-dimensional. The Committee's researchers talked to a lot of small businessmen but largely took them at their own estimation. The small business owner manager saw himself as disadvantaged by politicians, banks, large companies and local authorities, and misunderstood by the public at large. Making ends meet demanded virtually a total commitment of time and energy, with the rewards barely adequate. Trade unions were seen as another threat, despite the fact that their workers really wanted nothing to do with unions. Getting skilled, loyal workers was increasingly difficult, even though relations between boss and worker were seen as warm and friendly.

Current research on the owner manager and the entrepreneur offers a more rounded picture, with rather more warts, but carrying substantially more conviction. As Bolton suggested, small firm owner managers are far from randomly drawn from the population (Bolton Report, 1971: 22–25). On the whole, they tend to be relatively poorly educated and, often, running a small business is, in fact, an alternative to conventional forms of achievement in contemporary society. Achievement in the latter is increasingly defined as high office in a large organisation and this has become dependent upon paper qualifications in our credentialist society. For those who, for any reason, fail to obtain such qualifications, a small business is a major alternative path to success.

From time to time, it has been suggested that a new kind of entrepreneur was emerging in the 1970s – the R and D entrepreneur, as he has sometimes been labelled. The distinctive characteristic of this entrepreneur is an extended education, perhaps to PhD level in science or engineering, and especially in some area of new technology. He has also realised that his special knowledge can be converted into the basic asset of a new enterprise. This technological entrepreneur received considerable attention in the United States in the early 1970s (see, for example, Lyles, 1974). The extent to which he has emerged in Britain is uncertain (Balbin, 1980).

But one finding offered in the Bolton Report (23) which has been reiterated again and again, is that few owner managers make financial gain their key goal. Without exception, later studies of entrepreneurs and owner managers all underline this point (Boswell, 1973; Stanworth and Curran, 1973; Scase and Goffee, 1981 and 1982; Bannock, 1981: 36–38; Storey, 1982). Equally, the consensus of their findings is the stress placed on autonomy and independence as major personal goals, with the enterprise as the major arena for their expression.

These findings also accord with the main notions emerging in the recent revival of theorising and research into the *petit bourgeoisie* (Bechhofer and Elliott, 1976, 1978 and 1981; Scase and Goffee, 1982a; Scase, 1982). This 'uneasy stratum' or 'in-between' class in modern industrial society had been rather neglected, but it is now becoming accepted that it continues to survive strongly. Indeed, there are now over two million self-employed people in Britain – almost 9% of the labour force – and the change between 1979 and 1981 was the largest recorded biennial increase (Department of Employment, 1983: 55). Echoing the idea of the small businessman as socially marginal (Stanworth and Curran, 1973), this recent literature emphasises the continuing vulnerability of the *petit bourgeoisie* to change, booms, recessions and political decisions. Yet their great resilience as a stratum (Goldthorpe, Llewellyn and Payne, 1980) against formidable economic and political odds fully reflects their striving for autonomy and the value they place on this in their psychological make-up.

In turn, these dominant psychological characteristics of entrepreneurs and small firm owner managers have been repeatedly reported as manifesting themselves in a distinct managerial style. Kets de Vries (1977), in a summary of much of the available literature, argues that this managerial style is autocratic, impulsive, egocentric and essentially unpredictable. Forward planning is limited to the short term, and relations with employees are highly particularistic, ie involves a personal and sometimes idiosyncratic relationship.

Of course, we must beware of over-generalisation here. There is no single entrepreneurial or owner manager type but, rather, as research has indicated (for example, Stanworth and Curran, 1973 and 1976; Scase and Goffee, 1981 and 1982a), a range of entrepreneurial and owner manager identities which result from a subtle interaction between type of economic activity, period of establishment of the enterprise, level of success and whether the small firm executives are first generation entrepreneurs or those who have inherited ownership. But Kets de Vries has, in broad terms, drawn the central contrast between the informal, particularistic managerial style of small enterprise and the formal, bureaucratic administration of the typical large enterprise.

In addition, recent researchers have begun to explore specific subgroups within the owner manager class who are likely to offer a highly distinctive contribution to small enterprise formation and operation. For example, considerable interest is being expressed in ethnic minority-owned small businesses. The best known group among the latter are the Asians, many of whom arrived in Britain within the last two decades from East Africa. Already, a lively debate has emerged on the characteristics and future of Asian-owned small enterprise (Aldridge *et al.*, 1983).

Other ethnic minorities known to be substantially involved in small business activities are the Greek-Cypriots, Chinese and, to a lesser extent, the Afro-Caribbeans. None, however, have received a great deal of attention. Brook's (1982) survey of ethnic minority-owned businesses in the London borough of Lambeth showed that Afro-Caribbeans were much less likely to be involved in small enterprise than Asians. Partly, this is a difference in culture and experience; the Asians have a long history of involvement in small-scale business and have developed intra-community institutions to support their entrepreneurial activities.

Another specific group within the owner manager strata belatedly beginning to receive some attention are women small business owners. Women's contribution to entrepreneurship and the small enterprise has traditionally been much neglected. For example, in many small businesses nominally run by male owner managers, wives perform essential administrative and secretarial tasks, without which the business would probably fail (Scase and Goffee, 1982b; 103–107). But women are also frequently small business owners in their own right, particularly in areas such as hairdressing and retailing.

In one of the rare studies of women small business owners in Britain, Scase and Goffee (1982b) report that their motivations for setting up on their own were in many respects very similar to their male counterparts – independence, personal achievement and financial success. But there were also reasons connected with gender. For example, some had gone into business as a last resort as a solution to the problem of making a living as a single parent with children to care for. Small business ownership can be combined with running a home – often on the same premises – and flexible hours.

Women small business owners were often very conscious that their gender influenced their performance in their economic role. For instance, they sometimes found bank managers patronising and unsympathetic and believed this was because they were female. They were also conscious that in running a successful small business they ran the risk of being labelled 'unfeminine' or of developing the unattractive qualities of aggression and ruthlessness they perceived in some male small business owners. On the other hand, feminine charm and appeal were recognised as an asset in some business dealings and in relations with employees. Husbands did not contribute greatly to the business, reversing the findings on wives' contributions to male owned businesses.

Small business owner pressure groups

One of the most interesting developments of the 1970s was the emergence and growth of small business pressure groups. The Bolton Committee remarked on how extremely ineffective small business-men had been as a pressure group (Bolton Report, 1971: 93) and a glance at the list of individuals and organisations who made representations to the Committee (Bolton Committee, 1971: Appendix IV) shows a notable absence of such groups. All this has now changed and Britain's small businessmen are beginning to become a formidable pressure group.

This change was discussed in detail by McHugh (1979), who argued that this increasing representation has taken two main forms. First, an increase in activities on behalf of the small businessman by bodies such as the CBI, who claim to speak for industry as a whole. The CBI has always had an interest in the small firm, but the increase in independent associations claiming to be exclusively concerned with small businessmen's interests has, apparently, stimulated the CBI to greater awareness and action. Second, there has been a very public emergence of associations such as the National Federation of the Self-Employed and Small Businesses, established in 1974, which claimed a membership of 30,000 within its first six months. Other similar bodies are the Association of Independent Businesses, the Union of Independent Companies, the Forum of Private Business and the Small Business Bureau.

The lobbying tactics of these groups have often been crude and blatantly self-seeking, but they have experienced significant victories in winning concessions from governments and in making politicians of all parties much more positive towards the smaller business. For instance, the 1979 Conservative government increased the length of time before an employee could claim unfair dismissal from six months to one year and the Employment Act of 1980 provided that, for firms with 20 or fewer employees, the period would be two years (Westrip, 1982). Dispensations have been granted to small firms in relation to the Employment Protection Act maternity provisions and a great many small firms are now exempt from industrial training levies. Similar successes were achieved in the fields of taxation and finance in all the budgets since 1979, which followed similar favourable treatment from the previous Labour government, such as the abolition of capital transfer tax on businesses transferred within a family.

McHugh's analysis makes several key points. First, it is clear that for a variety of reasons, there is an inherent tendency for such groups to fragment. The implicit assumption underlying pressure group activities is that the constituency claimed to be represented is homogeneous with regard to outlook and views. But small business owner managers are a highly heterogeneous grouping with very differing interests, making it difficult for any single pressure group effecively to act on behalf of the small businessman and the self-employed.

Second, the representativeness of existing small business pressure groups may be questioned. Despite their successes, they have only recruited a relatively small proportion of their massive potential membership. The National Federation of the Self-Employed's own 1977 study of 7,500 members showed that the largest single grouping within their ranks were farmers, but that no other occupational group comprised more than 3% of the membership (McHugh, 1978: 66). As the National Federation for the Self-Employed's data also showed, there was a considerable membership wastage so that a lot of recruiting effort was required simply to maintain existing levels of membership. Other studies have shown that the small business owner manager is very often a non-joiner – his commitment to the value of independence frequently precludes collective behaviour (Scase and Goffee, 1980). Moreover, where the enterprise has become a consuming life interest, there may be little time, or desire, for outside activities.

Third, McHugh's data also show that many of the leaders of small business pressure groups, as well as many of the activists, have wider interests than the simple representation of the small business owner. These wider interests are often strongly ideological and are indicated by the close association between the leaders of small business pressure groups, such as the National Federation for the Self-Employed and groups such as the Freedom Association. Again, whether the majority of small business owner managers are strongly committed to such ideologies is open to question. They may be broadly sympathetic to the basic tenets of these ideologies, but whether they are in any way central to their practical life concerns of running their enterprise is another matter.

Moreover, as Bechhofer and Elliott (1981) point out, the claim to speak on behalf of 'little capitalists' has been made increasingly by voices other than small business pressure groups, thereby providing competition for the latter. For instance, several big companies have become economic and political sponsors for the small enterprise (as the activities of LEntA show, for example). The Conservative Party has attempted to recapture the support of the small enterprise owner with its own Small Business Bureau (established in 1976), as well as continuing the appointment of a minister with special responsibilities for the small enterprise. The other main parties also claim to favour the small enterprise.

These wider political and ideological changes add up to what Bechhofer and Elliott call the defence of a moral economy (1981: 190–91) through the emergence of a revived ideology of the new right, in which the small business is the embodiment of the principles of independence, thrift, straight dealing, ingenuity and hard work. This ideology re-moralises capitalism, attempting to halt the slide into the practices and structures which have been labelled 'the unacceptable face of capitalism' and seeks the return to a small-scale, competitive business order where multi-nationals and the domination of the big corporation would somehow vanish.

All told, these political and ideological shifts provide the most favourable ideological climate for the small business that has existed for decades in Britain and represents almost a total reversal of the position of 1971.

The small firm employee

As we noted earlier, the small firm employee was analysed in the Bolton Report entirely through the eyes of his or her employer. Because the small firm provided such a congenial work environment, employees were apparently willing to accept around 20% lower wages (Bolton Report, 21), as well as lower levels of fringe benefits. Conflict levels were also declared to be minimal (Bolton Report, 19). Other research (Ingham, 1970) reinforced this characterisation by introducing the notion of the self-selecting small firm worker whose main concern was with aspects of intrinsic job satisfaction most likely to be found in the small, rather than the large, firm.

Gradually, however, over the last decade this view of the small firm employee has changed and an altogether more refined and detailed characterisation has been established. It is also one which, like the view of the small firm employer examined in the previous section, has started to take account of the links between employment in the small enterprise and life in the wider society. This more recent and more complex view has several aspects. First, there is the meaning attached to working in the small enterprise, that is, what it means to the worker to work in the small, as opposed to the large, firm. Second, there are the findings concerning the social relations of the small enterprise, that is, the relations between worker and worker, but especially those between employee and owner manager. Thirdly, there are the links between employment experiences and membership of the wider community.

The meanings associated with small firm employment are a great deal more complex than was supposed in 1971. For instance, studies of occupational placement among manual workers generally indicate that their job seeking is usually carried out with little systematic knowledge and in a haphazard way: similar attitudes and behaviour have been found by research among small firm workers (Curran and Stanworth, 1979b). Small firm workers *are* more intrinsically minded than large firm workers, but this appears to be much more related to life cycle position and labour market dynamics than to the enterprise.

Small firm workers tend to be younger and are less likely to be married than workers in large firms. When such differences are controlled for, there appears little difference in levels of intrinsic mindedness among workers for a given industry, regardless of size of enterprise.

Job satisfaction among small firm workers also appears to be at odds with stereotype views. A recent study (Curran and Stanworth, 1981) suggests that once age and marital state are controlled for, differences are small in relation to size of enterprise and that, indeed, type of industry is much more important than size of enterprise. The influence of type of industry may actually be so great as to reverse the expected small firm/intrinsic satisfaction relationship.

The comparison of material reward levels in small and large firms has turned out to be even more difficult than the Bolton Report recognised. Differences in skill levels, experience, worker reliability, job titles, job content, etc., are considerable even between firms of similar size in the same industry. An association has been noted between low pay and working in a small enterprise, but the exact nature of the relationship is unclear (Pond, 1979). Workers' views, however, do not support the notion that intrinsic satisfaction compensates for lower material rewards. In the survey on job satisfaction noted above, although two out of three small firm workers believed their firm paid as well or better than any other firm they could work for (compared to 76% of the large firm workers), the majority also believed that the firm could and should pay more. The finding that small firms offered fewer fringe benefits – especially fringe benefits as of right – was confirmed.

Turning to research on social relations in the small enterprise, the most significant theoretical contribution to analysis here is that of Newby (1975 and 1977). This provides a subtle interpretation of the social relations of paternalistic capitalism, of which small firm worker owner manager relations are a major form. The heart of this interpretation is the insight that the major problem for the owner manager is the attempt to maintain an inherently contradictory relationship with subordinates, involving both differentiation and identification.

Differentiation involves the successful establishment and main-tenance of superior-subordinate relations conforming to the accept-able organisational form of the enterprise in our culture – a hierarchical, market constrained enterprise whose performance is ultimately measured in terms of profit. Identification requires a moral involvement in the enterprise by the employee and the existence of particularistic relations between employee and the owner manager. These are characteristic of the managerial style of the small firm owner manager, as well as an outcome of the face-to-face relations of this form of enterprise.

Such relations are inherently contradictory, because the logic of free enterprise dictates that the over-riding constraint over social relations in the enterprise will be impersonal, cash nexus, profit and loss considerations: personal relations must always, ultimately, be subordinate to these (see also Scott and Rainnie, 1982: 168). Yet the small business owner ideology stresses close personal social relations based on the assumption of a harmony of interests between the employer and employee. A good deal of the success of everyday social and economic relations in the enterprise will depend upon the good-will generated between employer and employees. The vulnerability of the small business to the ups and downs of the market, which produces sharp fluctuations in the economic constraints impingeing on the firm, is a continuous, unpredictable reminder of these contradictions for all those involved.

A study by the Policy Studies Institute for the Manpower Services Commission (Daniel, 1981) reported that workers in small firms were more likely than others to lose their jobs: 41% of the unemployed sample last worked for establishments employing less than 25 people. This is, of course, no less than might be expected of workers employed in secondary sectors of the economy which are more vulnerable to the forces of recession and change than larger firms.

Attitudinal data from small firm studies reflect these contradictions clearly. As the Bolton Report and its research reports, as well as earlier research (see, especially, Golby and Johns, 1971: 40–44; Scase and Goffee, 1982a, Ch. 5) implicitly revealed, small firm owner managers have divergent views on their relations with their employees. On the one hand, they report close, friendly and harmonious relations with 'their' workers but, on the other hand, they complain that they are unable to recruit and retain the kind of workers they seek, because of the 'pernicious effects of modern society' which had 'destroyed the will to work' and allowed the ordinary worker to be able to 'dictate his or her terms' to the employer.

For their part, small firm employees find their firm a friendly place in which to work – friendlier than they believe a large firm would be (Ingham, 1970; Batstone, 1975; Curran and Stanworth, 1979a). But some researchers have also reported that this view can go hand-in-hand with reservations about the strength of the relationship with their employer and the extent to which it transcended the basic cash nexus connection (Curran and Stanworth, 1979a). In other words, the contradictory elements in the small firm employment relationship are recognised on this side of the fence also.

The third area of research here – that concerning links between working in the small enterprise and membership of the wider social, economic and political order – has several facets. One of the most interesting, developed throughout the 1970s, is summed up in the notion of the segmented labour market (Bosanquet and Doeringer, 1973; Stolzenberg, 1978; Norris, 1978; Kreckel, 1980; Lawson, 1981; Scott and Rainnie, 1982; Hodson and Kaufman, 1982). Broadly, the argument developed here has been that workers and employers come to occupy more or less separate labour markets, rather than a single labour market. A major distinction has been drawn between primary and secondary labour markets. Primary labour markets consist of mainly large firms who recruit the cream of the labour market – the well-trained, well-qualified, experienced and reliable personnel – by offering them a combination of good wages, promotion opportunities and fringe benefits.

Secondary labour markets, on the other hand, consist of marginal firms, recruiting marginal workers. The workers will be less well-qualified and experienced, more likely to have had an unstable work record, to be younger, to be immigrant workers, or those without a trade union card. Women are also more likely to be found in the secondary labour market. Small firm employers who claimed difficulties in recruiting workers were, therefore, reporting the problems of recruiting in the secondary labour market, but their frequent belief that large firms suffer even worse problems is not entirely correct: rather, large firms suffer labour problems peculiar to the labour market in which they operate.

Labour market analysis of this kind has a bearing on the job creation potential of the small firm, which has been stressed by spokesmen for small firm pressure groups and politicians. A much cited study in relation to this aspect of the small firm is that of Birch (1979), which has widely (and mistakenly) been reported as showing that small firms in the United States created 4.5 million jobs, over two-thirds of all new jobs, in the period 1969–76. However, Fothergill and Gudgin (1979), reporting the findings from a British study of job generation, found that although small firms were a rather better bet for employment growth than large firms, large firms create a large number of new jobs, also. Put another way, while small firms may create many new jobs and more per unit of investment than large firms, they will only create a small percentage of *all* new jobs, because large firms play a more substantial role in the economy as a whole (CBI, 1980: 34–39; Bannock, 1981: 97). Storey (1981), in a similar study of small manufacturing firms in the North East, came to similar conclusions.

A further aspect of the worker/wider society relationship

concerns the community location of the enterprise. Batstone (1975) argued that community was the crucial determinant of worker/ management relations in his sample of small firms in semi-traditional Banbury. The 'ethos of small town capitalism' was, in his view, the source of the close relations and shared views of his small firm workers and employers. Norris (1978) has incorporated this into an analysis of the structural conditions required for the maintenance of paternalistic capitalism and Lawson (1982) has shown how such community factors can even reproduce elements of such relations in a large electronics firm. Conversely, the absence of community factors favourable to close worker/employer relations have been shown to be associated with more distant relations (Curran and Stanworth, 1979a). Overall, there can be little doubt that, nationally, the growth of the welfare state, the emergence of a national culture through the mass media, and particularly television, the increased emphasis on material consumption as the key to individual happiness, plus the increased domination of the economy by the large enterprise and the decline of the close-knit local community, are all factors undermining paternalistic capitalism.

Interest has also developed in the links between small firm employees and political attitudes and behaviour, an interest which parallels the more established interest in the ideology and politics of small firm owner managers. At the beginning of the 1970s the accepted view was that the small firm worker was a 'working class deferential', who viewed society as a natural social order governed by those who were born to authority. The deferential's place might be near the bottom of this order, but that was as things should be. He willingly accepted his lowly position in return for the psychological rewards and security of belonging to a fixed, natural order and the opportunities for association with higher status superiors. Such workers had relatively few contacts with other members of the working class, were unlikely to join trade unions and were likely to be Conservative Party supporter. In a study of political attitudes and Ingham (1969) broadly agreed with the idea of the small firm work environment having an independent effect on political attitudes, but his findings on actual voting behaviour were not entirely consistent with the idea of a small firm worker as a natural Conservative Party supporter. In a study of political attitudes and voting behaviour covering three of the General Elections of the 1970s, Curran (1980) found that there was little evidence for small firm workers having a deferential working class world view and that, politically, they were not strong supporters of the Conservatives. Rather, they were distinguished by the volatility of their political allegiances and their propensity not to vote at all, as compared to large firm workers. Like their employers, they were non-joiners, taking little part in voluntary associations of any kind, as compared to the large firm workers in the study (Curran, 1981).

The small business and the environment

Relations between the small business and its wider environment have been examined rather unevenly to date, although there is a good deal of speculation. For instance, both the local and national environments have been regarded as hostile to the small enterprise in the past but, more recently, there have been claims that this is being reversed. Certainly, indirect evidence in the early 1970s broadly supported these contentions. The Bolton Report (Ch. 6) concluded that Britain had the smallest small business sector of any private enterprise industrial society and Bannock (1981) reported that the picture had changed little since. He also noted (1981: 55) that 'the governments of most European countries as well as those of Japan and the United States have committed more effort and resources into promoting small business than Britain'.

However, pinning down the exact character of this assumed hostility to the small enterprise in Britain is not easy. For example, it has often been argued on behalf of small business owners that Britain's taxation system is highly unfavourable to the small business (Bannock, 1981: 107–121). But it is also possible to argue that, whatever may have been true before 1970, small enterprise owners and the self-employed are now among the most favoured in relation to the taxation system (Horner: 1983). In addition, although measuring tax evasion is difficult (O'Higgins, 1980), there are strong indications that the self-employed and small business owners are advantageously placed to break the law in this way and that many do so (McLoughlin, 1983). Indeed, the escape into Schedule D (with its opportunities for tax avoidance and evasion) may well be one of the strongest incentives towards setting up a small business, given the increasingly regressive character of the tax system for many of those employed by others (Kay and King, 1981).

Relations between the state and small business in Britain have recently undergone a fundamental change. Up to the 1970s the state's attitude to small enterprise was one of indifference: economic policy was formulated almost as if the economy consisted solely of large enterprises. But after the Bolton Report governments of all parties began to develop policies intended to encourage the small business. The Department of Industry under the 1979 Conservative government, for example, published a list of 98 measures designed specifically to assist small firms, ranging from the Loan Guarantee

Scheme, under which the state guaranteed 80% of loans to small businesses from financial institutions, to the elimination of a good deal of form filling by small enterprise owners (Department of Industry, 1983). These changes bring Britain more into line with other advanced industrial societies.

Unfortunately, research on the impact of these changes in government policies towards the small business has hardly begun. Whether, in fact, they will help the small firm, is unknown, but research on some of the changes, those connected with employment legislation, indicates that they are unlikely either to improve employer/worker relations in small firms or increase levels of employment in the small business sector (Westrip, 1982). As with many rapid changes in political policy fashions, decisions are made more on gut feelings or ideology than on the basis of careful research. In fact, in the case of the employment legislation changes, the 1979 Conservative government chose to disregard completely the findings of research sponsored by its own Department of Employment.

Probably the most publicised of the recent government policy innovations has been the Enterprise Zone, the creation of special economic environments designed to provide an ideal climate to promote the establishment of firms of all sizes, but especially small businesses. Firms in the zones are exempt from certain taxes, local authority rates, planning procedures and several other restrictions or requirements placed on businesses outside the zones. So far, eleven enterprise zones have been set up and a further 12 are scheduled (Department of Industry, 1983). Again, little research has been carried out on this policy innovation and, since they are intended as a 10-year experiment, it will be some time before a fair evaluation is possible. But the enterprise zone policy has none the less generated a good deal of theoretical discussion, much of it highly critical.

The *International Journal of Urban and Regional Research*, for example, published a set of papers in 1982 consisting of a statement and response by Peter Hall, the originator of the enterprise zone concept, and several critical commentaries (Harrison, 1982; Massey, 1982; Goldsmith, 1982). Hall himself appeared less than pleased with the way his ideas had been translated into policy. On the one hand, too many zones had been created and, on the other hand, individual zones were not free enough from the surrounding economy. What Hall had in mind originally were '... zones of fairly shameless free enterprise ... outside the scope of United Kingdom taxes, social services, industrial and other regulations' (1982: 417). The model was the Hong Kong of the 1960s translated to the depressed inner areas of Britain's declining cities.

Small businesses also have relations with local authorities, some of which have been eager to foster small enterprise and for much the same reasons – promoting employment and rejuvenating the economy generally. Many have appointed small enterprise promotion teams under one label or another, or supported freelance agencies promoting small firms. But Wilson (1982), in a survey of 158 local authority chief executives in England and Wales (carried out late in 1979), found that almost 40% of the 114 who responded had no small business programme at all. This figure may even be an understatement since, given who the respondents were, it might be expected that there would be a tendency to describe very modest or even nominal efforts as a 'programme'. In other words, the level of aid to small firms revealed by this study seems much lower than might be expected from the publicity local authorities have generated on this topic.

Also of interest were the differing views of the local authorities and the small firms on the latters' principal problems. The local authority respondents, for example, thought that a lack of suitable premises was a major problem but, except for the very smallest firms, respondents did not see premises as a central problem. The local authorities thought rates were a relatively unimportant problem, but the small firm respondents mentioned rates much more frequently, though they did not give them the overwhelming importance that many politicians and small business pressure groups have recently.

Conclusions

From this survey it is obvious that small business research in Britain is in an exceptionally healthy state, easily standing comparison with the level and quality of research emerging from other countries, including the United States. But the other two problems noted in the Introduction – disseminating the results of research to key users and bridging the gulf between researchers and those mainly involved in providing small business courses and counselling services – remain unsolved.

It would, of course, be wrong to imply that research findings by themselves provide all that is needed for effective small business education and counselling. Nonetheless, research offers an essential input into these activities. For instance, devising an overall approach to investment planning in the small manufacturing enterprise might well be totally misdirected if research findings on the typical approach to investment by small manufacturers are ignored (Hankinson, 1982). Or again, advising small firms on personnel practices and employee relations without a thorough understanding of owner manager attitudes to those they employ, is likely to be wasted breath if the suggested programmes are based on the 'best' practices of 'leading' employers (usually large firms). The above applies with equal force to small business policy-making. Policy makers in the main political parties, the civil service and local government, show considerable enthusiasm for promoting higher levels of small enterprise. But again, policy pronouncements often show little awareness of the results of the wealth of research discussed above. For instance, offering advice and aid through various bureaucratic outlets – government departments, local authorities, the clearing banks – often does not take account of the widespread distrust of the state and similar organisations which has been shown to be a key aspect of the outlook of so many small business owner managers. In other words, if official help to the small enterprise is to be effective, then attention has to be given to overcoming this distrust.

There are good reasons to suppose that the small business sector in Britain has enjoyed a revival over the last decade or so. The previous pessimistic assessment of the fate of the small business as a casualty of the emergence of post-industrial society seems to need replacing by one that suggests that, rather than being an anachronism, the small business sector is an integral and necessary part of the functioning of a modern economy. If small business researchers can get this message across to policy-makers and other decision-makers, the first step in achieving a balanced understanding of the role of small enterprise in contemporary industrial society will have been made.

Table 1

Small enterprise data, manufacturing industries, UK, 1963-1980

	No. of Small Enterprises (thousands)	As % of all Enterprises	Employment in Small Enterprises as % of Total	Net Output (by value) of Small Enterprises as % of Total
1963	65.7	94.1	21.3	18.0
1968	66.1	94.9	20.8	18.1
1970	70.9	95.2	21.3	18.5
1971	71.4	95.3	21.0	17.9
1972	69.0	95.4	21.5	18.4
1973	74.1	95.7	20.7	17.1
1974	81.1	96.0	21.5*	17.7*
1975	83.4	96.3	21.9*	18.0*
1976	86.3	96.5	22.6*	18.2*
1977	86.7	96.6	22.5*	18.7*
1978	87.2	96.7	22.8*	19.3*
1979	86.8	96.8	23.1*	19.5*
1980	87.4	96.9	24.3*	21.5*

Notes: 'Small' is defined as an enterprise employing less than 200 persons. Because the distribution of manufacturing firms is highly skewed, a definition of 'small' as firms employing less than 100 would not proportionately alter these figures. For example, in 1979 enterprises employing less than 100 were 93.9% of all manufacturing enterprises and in 1980, 94.2%. They employed 17.5%* of all manufacturing workers in 1979 and 18.8%* in 1980. They contributed 14.6%* of net manufacturing output in 1979 and 16.6%* in 1970.
*Data based on establishment not enterprise figures.
Because of changes in the ways in which the data are collected and classified, caution has to be exercised in interpreting the results.

SOURCES: Interim Report of the Committee to Review the Functioning of Financial Institutions, Cmnd. 7503, HMSO 1979, Tables 2.1, 2.2 and 2.3. Reports of the Censuses of Production, 1974–75 and for the years 1976 to 1980, all published HMSO, 1978–1983.

References

Aldrich, H. *et al.*, 'Ethnic Advantage and Minority Business Development' in Ward, R. and Jenkins, R. (eds.) *Ethnic Business*, Cambridge University Press, 1983.

Bannock, G., *The Smaller Business in Britain and Germany*, London, Wildwood House, 1976.

Bannock, G., *The Economics of Small Firms, Return from the Wilderness*, Oxford, Blackwell, 1981.

Batstone, E. V., *Aspects of Stratification in a Community Context: A Study of Class Attitudes and the 'Size Effect'*, Ph.D. thesis, University of Wales, 1969.

Batstone, E. V., 'Deference and the Ethos of Small Town Capitalism', in Bulmer, M. (ed.) *Working-Class Images of Society*, London, Routledge and Kegan Paul, 1975.

Bechhofer, F. and Elliott B., 'Persistence and Change: the Petite Bourgeois in Industrial Society', *European Journal of Sociology*, Vol. XVII, 1976.

Bechhofer, F. and Elliott, B. (eds), *The Petite Bourgeoisie, Comparative Studies of the Uneasy Stratum*, London, Macmillan, 1981.

Belbin, R. M., 'Launching New Enterprises, Some Fresh Initiatives for Tackling Unemployment', *Department of Employment Gazette*, Vol. 88, No. 4, 1980.

Bell, D., *The Coming of Post-Industrial Society*, London, Heinemann, 1974.

Birch, D., 'The Job Generation Process', M.I.T. Programme on Neighbourhood and Regional Change, Cambridge, Mass., M.I.T., 1979.

Bosanquet, N. and Doeringer, P. B., 'Is There a Dual Labour Market in Britain?', *Economic Journal*, Vol. 83, 1973.

Boswell, J., *The Rise and Decline of Small Firms*, London, Allen and Unwin, 1973.

Brewers' Society (The), *Beer Facts 1982*, London, 1983.

Brooks, A., *Black Business in Lambeth*, Directorate of Town Planning, London Borough of Lambeth, 1982.

CBI, *Smaller Firms in the Economy*, London, 1980.

Chaplin, P., *Co-operatives in Contemporary Britain*, in Stanworth, J. *et al.* (eds.), 1982.

Collins, O. F., Moore, D. G., with Unwalla, D. B., *The Enterprising Man*, East Lancing, Michigan State University Press, 1964.

Curran, J., 'The Political World of the Small Firm Worker', *Sociological Review*, Vol. 28, No. 1, February, 1980.

Curran, J., 'Class Imagery, Work Environment and Community: some Further Findings and a Brief Comment', *British Journal of Sociology*, Vol. XXXII, No. 1, March, 1981.

Curran, J. and Stanworth, J., 'Worker Involvement and Social Relations in the Small Firm', *Sociological Review*, Vol. 27, No. 2, May, 1979a.

Curran, J. and Stanworth, J., 'Self-Selection and the Small Firm Worker – A Critique and an Alternative View', *Sociology*, Vol. 13, No. 3, September, 1979b.

Curran, J. and Stanworth, J., *A New Look at Job Satisfaction in the Small Firm*, Human Relations, Vol. 34, No. 5, May, 1981.

Daniel, W. W., *The Unemployed Flow*, Stage I Interim Report, London, Policy Studies Institute, 1981.

Department of Employment, 'How Many Self-Employed?', *Employment Gazette*, Vol. 91, February, 1983.

Department of Industry, 'Summary of Government Measures of Benefit to Small Firms', February, 1983 and *How to Make Your Business Grow*, April, 1983.

Feige, E. L. and McGee, R. T., 'Tax Revenue Losses and the Unobserved Economy in the U.K.', *Journal of Economic Affairs*, Vol. 2, No. 3, 1982.

Financing of Small Firms (The), *Interim Report of the Committee to Review the Functioning of Financial Institutions*, Cmnd. 7503, London, HMSO, 1979 (The Wilson Report).

Fothergill, S. and Gudgin, G., *The Job Generation Process in Britain*, London, Centre for Environmental Studies, 1979.

Galbraith, J. K., *The New Industrial State*, Hammondworth, Penguin, 1969.

Gershuny, J., *After Industrial Society? The Emerging Self-Service Economy*, London, Macmillan, 1978.

Gershuny, J. and Pahl, R. E., 'Britain in the Decade of the Three Economies', *New Society*, 9 January, 1980.

Golby, C. W. and Johns, G., *Attitude and Motivation, Committee of Inquiry on Small Firms*, Research Report No. 7, London, HMSO, 1971.

Goldsmith, W. W., 'Enterprise Zones: If They Work, We're in Trouble', *International Journal of Urban and Regional Research*, Vol. 6, No. 3, 1982.

Goldthorpe, J. H. with Llewellyn, C. and Payne, C., *Social Mobility and Class Structure in Modern Britain*, Oxford, Clarendon Press, 1980.

Hall, P., 'Enterprise Zones: a Justification' and 'Response', *International Journal of Urban and Regional Research*, Vol. 6, No. 3, 1982.

Hankinson, A., *The Investment Problem, a Study of Investment Behaviour of South Wessex Small Engineering Firms, 1979–1982*, Poole, Dorset Institute of Higher Education, 1982.

Harrison, B., 'The Politics and Economics of the Urban Enterprise Zone Proposal: a Critique', *International Journal of Urban and Regional Research*, Vol. 6, No. 3, 1982.

Hodson, R. and Kaufman, R. L., 'Economic Dualism: a Critical Review', *American Sociological Review*, Vol. 47, December, 1982.

Horner, J., 'The Latest Tax Haven: Small Business', *In Business*, Issue 44, 25 March, 1983.

Ingham, G. K., 'Plant Size, Political Attitudes and Behaviour', *Sociological Review*, Vol. 17, November, 1969.

Ingham, G. K., *Size of Industrial Organisation and Worker Behaviour*, Cambridge University Press, 1970.

Institute of Petroleum (The), *Petroleum Retail Outlet Survey*, London, 1983.

Kay, J. and King, M. R., *The British Tax System*, London, Oxford University Press, 2nd edition, 1981.

Kets De Vries, M. F. R., 'The Entrepreneurial Personality: a Person at the Crossroads', *Journal of Management Studies*, Vol. 14, No. 1, January, 1977.

Kirby, D., 'Training and Advisory Services for the Small Retail Business – the Case for Government Action' in Stanworth, J. *et al.* (eds.), 1982.

Kirby, D., statistics estimated by Retail Research Unit, Department of Geography, University of Wales (Director: David Kirby), 1983.

Kreckel, R., 'Unequal Opportunity Structure and Labour Market Segmentation', *Sociology*, Vol. 14, No. 4, 1980.

Lawson, T., 'Paternalism and Labour Market Segmentation Theory' in Watkinson, F. (ed.), *Essays in the Dynamics of Labour Markets*, Cambridge University Press, 1982.

Liles, P. R., 'Who are the Entrepreneurs', *MSU Business Topics*, Winter, 1974.

Lockwood, D., 'Sources of Variation in Working Class Images of Society', *Sociological Review*, Vol. 14, No. 3, November, 1966.

Massey, P., 'Enterprise Zones: a Political Issue', *International Journal of Urban and Regional Research*, Vol. 6, No. 3, 1982.

Mayer, K. B. and Goldstein, S., *The First Two Years: Problems of Small Firm Growth and Survival*, Washington, Small Business Administration, 1961.

McClelland, D. C., *The Achieving Society*, New York, Van Nostrand, 1961.

McHugh, J., 'The Self-Employed and the Small Independent Entrepreneur', in King, R. and Nugent, N. (eds.) *Respectable Rebels, Middle Class Campaigns in the 1970s*, London, Hodder and Stoughton, 1979.

McLoughlin, J., 'VAT Frauds Cost up to £500m', *The Guardian*, 21 May, 1983.

Motor Agents' Association, figures supplied by Neal Marshall, Statistician, Legal and Commercial Department, 1983.

Newby, H., 'The Deferential Dialectic', *Comparative Studies in Society and History*, Vol. 17, No. 2, 1975.

Newby, H., 'Paternalism and Capitalism' in Scase, R. (ed.) *Industrial Society; Class, Cleavage and Control*, London, Allen and Unwin, 1977.

Newby, H., Bell, C., Rose, D. and Saunders, P., *Property, Paternalism and Power*, London, Hutchinson, 1978.

Norris, G. M. 'Industrial Paternalistic Capitalism and Local Labour Markets', *Sociology*, Vol. 12, No. 3, 1978.

O'Higgins, M., *Measuring the Black Economy*, London, Outer Circle Policy Unit, 1980.

Parkin, F., *Class Inequality and Political Order: Social Stratification in Capitalist and Communist Societies*, London, Paladin, 1972.

Pond, C., 'Small Change; Small Firms, Labour Law and Low Pay', *Low Pay Unit Bulletin*, No. 29, October, 1979.

Rothwell, R. and Zegweld, W., *Innovation in the Small and Medium Sized Firm*, London, Frances Pinter, 1982.

Scase, R., 'The Petty Bourgeoisie and Modern Capitalism: a Consideration of Recent Theories', in Giddens, A. and MacKenzie, G. (eds.) *Social Class and the Division of Labour*, Cambridge University Press, 1982.

Scase, R. and Goffee, R., *The Real World of the Small Business Owner*, London, Croom Helm, 1980.

Scase, R. and Goffee, R., ' "Traditional" Petty Bourgeois Attitudes: the Case of the Self-Employed Craftsmen', *Sociological Review*, Vol. 29, No. 4, 1981.

Scase, R. and Goffee, R., *The Entrepreneurial Middle Class*, London, Croom Helm, 1982a.

Scase, R. and Goffee, R., 'Why Some Women Decide to Become Their Own Bosses', *New Society*, 9 September, 1982b.

Scott, M. and Rainnie, A., 'Beyond Bolton – Industrial Relations in the Small Firm', in Stanworth, J. *et al* (eds.), 1982.

Small Firms – Report of the Committee of Inquiry on Small Firms, London, Cmnd. 4811, HMSO, 1971 (The Bolton Report).

Stanworth, J. *et al.* (eds.), *Perspectives on a Decade of Small Business Research, Bolton Ten Years On*, Aldershot, Gower Press, 1982.

Stanworth, J. and Curran, J., *Management Motivation in the Smaller Business*, Epping, Gower Press, 1973.

Stanworth, J. and Curran, J., 'Growth and the Small Firm – An Alternative View', *Journal of Management Studies*, Vol. 13, No. 2, May, 1976.

Storey, D. J., 'New Firm Formation, Employment Change and the Small Firm: the Case of Cleveland County', *Urban Studies*, Vol. 18, 1981.

Storey, D. J., *Entrepreneurship and the New Firm*, London, Croom Helm, 1982.

Thornley, J., *Workers' Co-operatives: Jobs and Dreams*, London, Martin Robertson, 1981.

Westrip, A., 'A Study of Research into the Effects of Employment Legislation on Small Firms' in Watkins, D., Stanworth, J. and Westrip, A. (eds.), *Stimulating Small Firms*, London, Gower Publishing, 1982.

Wilson, P., 'Local Authority Assistance to Small Firms' in Watkins, D. *et al.* (eds.), 1982.

Notes

1. The most comprehensive recent bibliography on the small business is: P. Dowell (ed.) *The London Business School Small Business Bibliography*, London Graduate School of Business Studies, Second Edition, 1983.

2. The only academic journal concerned exclusively with small business research currently published in Britain is the *International Small Business Journal*.

3. This chapter is an edited version of a paper presented to the Seventh National Small Business Management Teachers' Programme, London, July, 1983.